Closing the Circle

An American Family in China

Elsie Hayes Landstrom

QED Press
Fort Bragg, California

Closing the Circle: An American Family in China
Copyright © 1998 by Elsie Hayes Landstrom

For information, phone (707) 964-9520. For bookseller and library discounts or VISA and MasterCard orders, please call 800-773-7782. Or write to:

QED Press
155 Cypress Street, Fort Bragg CA 95437

Library of Congress Cataloging-in-Publication Data

Landstrom, Elsie H.
    Closing the circle : an American family in China / Elsie Hayes Landstrom.
       p.   cm.
    ISBN 0-936609-38-9
    1. Landstrom, Elsie H. — Biography.   2. Authors, American —20th century — Biography.   3. Missions — China.   I. Title.
PS3562.A4833C46   1998
226'.0092—dc20
[B]   98-17397
                                       CIP

Cover design by Theresa Whitehill, Colored Horse Studio

Book production by Cypress House

Printed in the United States of America by Gilliland Printing

First Edition

2 4 6 8 9 7 5 3 1

To the memory of my parents
Helen Wolf Hayes and Paul Goodman Hayes
and to that of my husband
Norman Landstrom

Helen Wolf and Paul Hayes in Nagasaki, Japan, enroute to China in 1921.

Paul Goodman Hayes, eighty-seven years old, at the celebration of his sixty years in the ministry, 6 November 1977, at Lake Harriet United Methodist Church, Minneapolis, Minnesota.

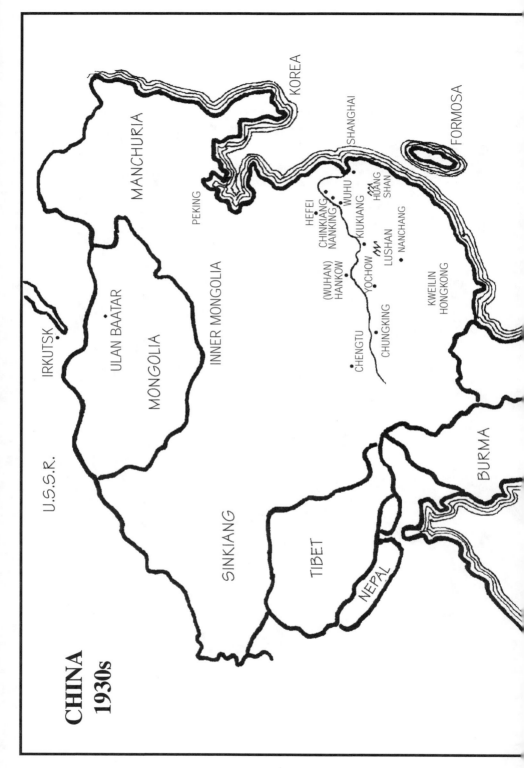

CHINA
1930s

U.S.S.R.

IRKUTSK

ULAN BAATAR

MONGOLIA

SINKIANG

INNER MONGOLIA

MANCHURIA

KOREA

PEKING

SHANGHAI

FORMOSA

WUHU
HEFEI
CHINKIANG
NANKING
KIUKIANG
HUANG SHAN
NANCHANG
(WUHAN)
HANKOW
YOCHOW
LUSHAN
CHUNGKING
CHENGTU
KWEILIN
HONGKONG

TIBET

NEPAL

BURMA

1 inch = 150 miles

SHANTUNG

HONAN

KIANGSU

ANHWEI

WUHSI

HEFEI

CHINKIANG

NANKING

SOOCHOW

SHANGHAI

SILIANSHAN

MAANSHAN
TSAISHICHI

CHAOHSIEN

WUHU

WANCHI

HUANGHU

HANGCHOW

HUPEH

ANKING

NINGKWAFU

TAIPING

KIUKIANG

HUANGSHAN

CHINGTECHEN

TUNKI

YOCHOW

LUSHAN

CHEKIANG

NANCHANG

KIANGSI

CHANGSHA

HUNAN

Acknowledgments

In addition to my parents, I am indebted to others of their generation who were my childhood friends. Those who shared memories with me, or sent me their own memoirs, include Bertha E. Cassidy, Walter Haskell, Lucile T. Libby and Hyla S. Watters.

Jonathan D. Spence read an early version of my manuscript, when I was at a loss to know how to proceed. He made the one comment that touched its core and pointed the direction. To him I owe a great deal. His rereading of the book in its last incarnation is most generous, especially at a time when he was finishing his eleventh book on Chinese history and culture, the recently published *God's Chinese Son,* a remarkable study of the Taiping uprising. Jonathan Spence is Sterling Professor of History at Yale University.

Three friends have given exceptionally gracious readings with informed criticisms. Oscar Armstrong, son of Southern Presbyterian missionaries, spent nearly twenty years in China. Now retired as a career Foreign Service Officer specializing in Asia, especially China, he is founder and editor of the quarterly, *The China Connection,* and teaches adult courses loosely affiliated with American University in Washington, D.C. Fred W. Drake, professor of Chinese history at the University of Massachusetts, has written books on China, taken numerous student groups to China in recent years, established a productive relationship with Chinese scholars and is president of the New England Conference of the Association for Asian Studies. Edward B. Gulick, Emeritus Professor of history at Wellesley College, has recently published an impressive memoir of his teaching years in wartime China.

Others who have helped in various ways include Margaret Berry, Roberta Brown Castro, Jean Esser, Elizabeth Gulick, Doris Karsell, Deane Lee, Virginia Steward Neuhauser, Aina Niemela, Rear Admiral (U.S. Navy Retired) Kemp Tolley, Peter Wan and Wang Hui-ming.

For events of 1927 I drew heavily on letters from Anna M. Jarvis found among my mother's papers. I used standard histories to sketch in the historical background, plundered files in the Yale China Records Project and United Methodist Church archives for the mission story. The 1930 *Directory of Protestant Missions in China* and various issues of *The Chinese Recorder* were valuable in helping me to understand the different viewpoints of missionaries and my father's written contributions to the evolving thinking of the times. For romanizations of Chinese words I have retained Wade-Giles and Atlas spellings in use at the time.

Most of the photographs are from my parents' albums, supplemented by those taken by Howard A. Smith (loaned to me by his son, Ray H. Smith). Others loaned by Carrel Morgan and the General Commision on Archives and History, the United Methodist Church.

Once again Shel Horowitz and Dina Friedman transferred manuscript to word processor, while those at QED Press — Cynthia Frank, John Fremont, Pradha Bush, Marco McClean, Sherry LeRoy and Charles Maden — shepherded the book through publication.

Errors are all my own.

We shall not cease from exploration
And the end of all our exploring
Will be to arrive where we started
And know the place for the first time.
—T.S. Eliot

Contents

Pagoda at Nanling, Anwhei

Howard A. Smith

From the Huts
Among the Willows

BEFORE ASCENDING A HEIGHT
YOU MUST START AT THE BOTTOM.
— CHINESE SAYING

More than sixty years ago, when I lived in the town of Wuhu on the banks of the Yangtze River two hundred sixty miles almost due west of Shanghai, Hsiao Pao and Hsiao Shih, two boys who lived in mud huts among the willows that lined the dike along the river, came over our compound wall to play with me.

Hsiao Pao taught and then always beat me at shuttlecock. Hsiao Shih's skill with marbles won him my Moonstone and Blue Treasure. Once, soon after we first started to play together, when I beat them at table tennis, they brought me a baby rabbit to cuddle, then took it away. Moments later its bloody head sailed over the wall to land at my feet. When they learned, a long time later, that I was to leave Wuhu, Hsiao Pao's face went blank, Hsiao Shih's lean one blanker; then they went away and when they came again they put into my hands a miniature deep-red vase that was smooth and cool to hold, its line from neck to base a gentle curve that comforted the eye. In it was a single starflower, probably stolen from my mother's garden.

Between these two events, which came to symbolize for me a wholeness binding together loveliness with the ugly, the boys let me tag along with them into their world. Their huts among the willows, smoky and dim, where ragged infants and pigs and chickens wandered in and out, drew me more and more frequently during the years when other foreign

1

children were in short supply. So it was that many of the tales I heard, the smell and taste, the sound, touch and rhythm of life I knew were not fully those of my parents. To Hsiao Pao and Hsiao Shih I owe much of the vision with which I see my world.

But I did not realize that until 1978 when my father retired for the third time at the age of eighty-eight. With my mother he sorted papers and household effects preparing to move from their home to an apartment, and sent me twelve journals he had kept while in China. Enthralled by the story they told, jarred by the realization of how much I did not yet understand about my parents, of how differently I had experienced our life in China, I was driven to get back in touch with friends we had seen seldom or not at all since we left China in 1935, to read their books, their letters, their reports to their mission boards. I became aware that some members of my generation, children of China Protestant missionaries in the 1920s and 1930s, were asking the questions I asked.

I found many stories of China missionaries whose zeal hardly flagged during those chaotic years in which China fought her way into the modern world. I found increasing recognition of the value of mission work in China on the part of the historians. But most stories petered out in irony: although the missionaries laid the foundations for many of the programs carried to fruition by the Communists, China saw them as agents of foreign imperialism and threw them out.

My parents' story did not fit easily into the general pattern. It differed from those that grew out of heroic events. They were not yet in China when the Boxer troubles exploded in 1900. They were on furlough in America when Chiang Kai-shek marched on the Northern Expedition to try to subdue the warlords and unify the country in 1927. They had been withdrawn from China before Japanese aggression spread into a general war in 1937, before the bitter Chinese civil war reached its climax.

My parents' story differed from those who pioneered in the treatment of cholera and leprosy and tuberculosis, from those who established cooperatives as an alternative to economic exploitation, from those who engineered flood control measures, who established great universities and medical schools and sought to eradicate opium and slavery and famine.

My parents' generation, filled with disillusion following the First World War, rallied around the conviction that it was up to each of them, individually, to bring Christ's spirit of love and hope into every human heart. Thousands responded to the call of the Student Volunteer Movement for Foreign Missions, which recruited American college students to work in China, India, the Middle East, Africa, the islands of the Pacific, and they fanned out over the world eager to save it.

My father had decided to become a missionary long before he heard of the Student Volunteer Movement during his college days, when he became one of its campus leaders. His generation failed in its purpose, but that they went to China in astonishing numbers is a fact worth relating to the magnitude of human suffering they found there. The impact they made is an undeniable part of the complex world we have inherited.

My father went to China as an evangelist, but he was assigned work as an administrator. He was a man of conviction who changed his views as he became aware of Chinese realities and worked steadily to turn mission work into Chinese work. He was a leader in the painful conflict within the Protestant mission body between those who believed that Christianity in its Western garb was the answer to China's vast problems, and those who did not.

Administration and theology are hardly the stuff of high drama, but I thought my parents' story ought to be told and urged my father to write it. I longed to hear the sound of his typewriter, the music of my childhood that lulled me to sleep while he labored over mission reports, sermons, letters and articles of passionate concern to him as he surveyed the unjust and suffering world about him. I wanted to see his eyes thinking, remembering, flashing with the power of his convictions. But he was eighty-eight. The macula of his left eye was deteriorating. He read and his eyes filled and streamed. Arthritis in his back moved him restlessly about. He was not convinced of the worth of what he had done.

Slowly the excitement of ideas and events long forgotten reawoke, and his resistance to my campaign weakened as I photocopied pages from his journals and sent them to him, and played back for him taped conversations about our lives in China. Finally he was willing to write, but only in the third person, and he sketched out a title page with my name on it as author. This troubled me. Suddenly I realized that I did not go to China as a missionary, I was born there. My experience of God was compelling, but had none of the marks of Christianity.

What might seem obvious — that my early world was entirely different from that in which my parents had been nurtured — had not been obvious to me at all.

Why had it taken me so long to realize this? It was partly because, under the influence of the psychological thinking of my generation, I had interpreted the differences between my parents and myself entirely in terms of the normal conflicts between the generations, the clash of our differing personalities. The job of understanding and reconciliation I set out on in my teens continued and deepened through the years, but seemed not to yield that final insight to close the gap between us. I remained unaware of the powerful influence China had had in shaping me.

It also took a long time for me to realize how disconnecting an experience had been our shift to America followed by decades when our two countries had nothing to do with each other. Our American life buried our Chinese life.

In China my mother spoke often of "home" and "going home," but America was a green shape on the map to me, the place my friend Dottie Brown and I tried to dig a hole to in the back yard and found instead silver spoons hidden by missionaries of an earlier day. It was the place that sent us boxes of shoes and dresses that seldom fit, with small surprises like a miniature celluloid doll or gray plaster cat tucked in among them. But home? Throughout my years in America my eye has been on a stealthy search of every house that catches my attention: does it suggest the home I hadn't the time to outgrow?

When I reached America I stuck out like a camelopard. Again and again I was asked to "tell about China," yet ridiculed for my foreign ways, until I found myself sidling up to the crippled and dark-skinned for comfort. I complied with requests to tell about China until the day a "slam book," that went the rounds of the classroom in a plot to take everyone down a peg or two, yielded the words "stuck up" following my name. A paralyzing shyness deepened even further and hid beneath a gay social manner copied from my mother. I turned my back on China, determined to live as indistinguishable a life from those around me as possible.

It took years to build a precarious self-esteem, especially before it became commonplace for Americans to travel abroad. When my friends first returned to tell in disbelief how it was they found people living in Africa, the Middle East and, finally, in China, I was startled by their shock and began to realize what it was I had taken for granted. Today I give thanks that I know what it means to become a stranger in a foreign land, for such knowledge is to hold in one's hand one of the keys to the heart of our world. I came out from hiding when it was safe to do so, although our children helped start the process by asking for "stories when you were little," and were disappointed to learn they were not half-Chinese.

Today I am comfortably aware that it is the American experience to search for one's roots in other lands. But there are still times when I note a look pass over the face of someone who has just learned of my missionary background, a look that tells me I am suspect. It took a while to translate this look into the realization that it was connected to a stereotype image of "missionary." To see myself reflected in this way forced me to examine the image, to peel back layers of self-deception that separated me from my parents as I discovered how deeply embedded the stereotype is in the American experience.

I have been among those to have spoken scornfully of the do-gooder, unaware of his presence within myself; I have been among those to play out my good intentions untroubled by awareness of harm I might do. I came to realize how often we Americans are filled with blind zeal, absolute conviction that our way is The Way and exportable for the good of those who haven't our brand of wisdom; that this is exactly what we deplore in the stereotype we have of the missionary. Alive and well in our society, the missionary is clearly visible in those who try to reshape it to be more responsive to human need. By becoming aware of this figure in ourselves and realizing his blind spots and his true vision, perhaps we can learn to link the missionary's powerful sense of commitment to what is nourishing and beneficial for our own and the world community.

As my search into the story of my family in China revealed more and more discrepancies between my memories and those of my parents, I knew I had to return to China to close the broken circle of my life. I found a language tutor, haunted the Chinese embassy in Washington, bombarded the Chinese government with ideas to tutor students in English or work as a "polisher," as they call copy editors on foreign language journals. But I had no institutional connections. In 1978, 1979 and 1980 the door to China was open, but not yet to individuals entering on their own.

Seven times the Chinese government rejected me, while I kept alert to any opportunity to reach China other than the three-week tour that would bypass the scenes of my childhood and fail to make the vital connections I needed.

When I learned that an experimental group of Columbia University students was to spend the summer of 1980 at the East China Normal University in Shanghai, I applied to go with them. The Shanghai faculty, intrigued by the idea that anyone over thirty might be able to learn, accepted me. It was a tough summer, hot, humid, devoted to long hours of language study. It was an uncertain summer of delays and anxieties while my request to return to Wuhu was weighed and debated.

Back in America I launched into shaping my father's book, only to have it turn in unexpected directions. My own questions kept getting in the way. What propelled my parents to leave their strict German-Irish homes in Pennsylvania and travel half-way around the world to change the hearts and minds of a people known to resist the efforts of the most expert persuaders? What was it like for my parents to go to China, and what did they actually do there? What was the story of the Wuhu Hospital in which our family played a part? What happened to the Wuhu story after we stepped out of it? Would I want to live in China today, or could I possibly want to live in the China I knew in my childhood? I maintain tenuous ties to a Quaker meeting, but am not a practicing Christian as my parents understand that to mean. Why not? How can those of us in the East and the West ever understand each other when someone with my background in both cultures finds it so difficult?

Unable to see clearly what I was doing, advised to quit by a number of publishers who told me that "missionaries don't sell," yet unable to give up, I went to friends for help and learned I was writing a book of my own. This discovery was a relief, but when you write a book you hadn't intended to write and start it at the age of nearly sixty, you need all the help you can get. My friends gallantly reread as I slowly turned my focus around.

As this memoir developed I became anxious about the ways in which it departed from my father's ideas for it. I placed it hesitantly in his hands, but need not to have doubted his generosity of spirit. He read and returned it saying, "It is *your* book, and you must feel free to write it in your own way."

This, then, is the story unearthed as I searched for answers to my questions. Not my story. Not my father's. It is both our stories, woven into those of China and our mission as I tried to make sense of my early world. It is a story filtered through childhood memories that have themselves been altered by the experiences and insights of the years. Errors of fact are, of course, my own, but are perhaps less important than the persons and times evoked. In the telling it has become both record and process of an inward search and healing.

Dr. Robert E. Brown, Superintendent of Wuhu General Hospital 1926-1939, and his family: Mae Willis Brown, their sons Harold and Willis, and daughter Dorothea Roberta (Dottie). Dr. Brown built the new hospital in 1926-1927 after the old one burned down. During the war with Japan he protected refugees who sought shelter in the compound, then was called to coordinate the work of mission and government hospitals followed by service on the Burna Road for which he was decorated by Chiang Kai-shek.

My mother and myself in 1925 visiting our neighbors. This is the only photograph I have of those huts among the willows and the friends who became so important to me in later years.

Paul G. Hayes

Wuhu on the Yangtze

LOVE FOR HOME INCLUDES THE CROWS.

— CHINESE SAYING

One sweltering afternoon when I was eight or ten, my friend Dottie Brown and I stretched out flat by the saloon skylight of a British Yangtse steamer where we could watch the British, Russian, Chinese, Japanese, American and Portuguese grownups below at tea. A small punkah-puller sat cross-legged and half asleep on the floor behind the drape, automatically working the rope that kept a mild air stirring over the tea table.

Bored with talk of Red bandits and Chiang Kai-shek, we remembered a white-painted metal partition adorned with intriguing levers toward the bow of the steamer, below the wheelhouse. The adults safely corralled for the moment, we sneaked down to look at those levers, pulled one, and when nothing happened exchanged a glance in which Dottie became captain and I steersman responding to her orders. Suddenly the anchor chain ran out, and the steamer, plowing full speed upriver, abruptly caught on a mud bar. Subsequent events, liberally laced with an apoplectic captain, amused sailors and horror-struck parents, are best left veiled.

Dottie and I were frequently the only foreign children on Ichishan, the mission compound that rose on a hill from the banks of the Yangtze outside the walled city of Wuhu, where her father, Robert E. Brown, was superintendent of the Wuhu General Hospital. Dottie was a year or two older than I, often away at school or bedridden with a mysterious illness that kept her bluish and thin but never diminished her sense of her own value, her small face a resolute miniature of her father's as she bossed around this willing accomplice.

The Hill, as Ichishan was known, was the scene of most of our adventures, and all too often we ran our ship of fun aground. We climbed the hospital electric transformer after a rainstorm and refused to come down for a distraught Lao Wang, the hospital engineer, who tried to warn us of dangers in heavy wires plunging through a nearby puddle. For this discourtesy my father marched me off to ask Lao Wang's pardon.

We practiced Morse Code with flashlights on the flat hospital roof so that we could show off our new skill to the chief surgeon, Hyla S. Watters, who had taught it to us. When we flashed a dim SOS back and forth, it was picked up by an alert signal officer on the H.M.S. *Gnat* riding at anchor midstream in the Yangtze. An armed landing party was dispatched to rescue our mission, and it took representatives of the governments of Great Britain, the United States and China to disentangle misunderstandings we had set loose.

We ran the hospital milk goats dry when, pretending to be cowboys (the American West symbolized adventure to us), we herded them into a stampede across Western ranges. As pioneers weary from the rigors of covered wagon travel, we cooked potatoes on a small fire that we hid from hostile Indians by building it under Hyla Doc's porch. Alarmed Chinese notified Hyla Doc that we had set her house on fire, and she came flying out of surgery in mask, gown and gloves, shouting up a fire brigade. We threw stones at the home of the Chinese surgeon (for what reason I have no memory, most probably as part of our Wild West inventions, as Dr. K.B. Liu was a good friend) for which I was made to fall on my knees beside my father afterwards and ask God's pardon, then walk straight up to the house and ask the same of Dr. Liu.

We filched broken syringes from the hospital dump to play doctor and built a playhouse from a pile of bricks used eventually to build a second wing to the hospital. We swung out over the hillside toward the river on thick ropes of wisteria, learning to skin-the-cat in air heavy with the grapey scent of huge clusters of blue blossoms that framed the glint of sun on waves below. With the doctors who enjoyed hunting deer and pheasant, we tagged along to make ourselves useful as retrievers, dodging wild boar by climbing trees. We listened to Dr. Brown's crystal radio set that sported an elegant trumpet-shaped speaker, and took turns wearing its headphones, spellbound by the static which we believed to be the "music of the spheres" we sang about on Sundays.

The few times Dottie Brown was in Wuhu during the school year we did sums and composition with Mother, read history and traced maps of Egypt, Palestine, Greece, Europe and the United States, locating rivers and cities to become familiar during long months of travel to America in later years, but we would have had a hard time finding the Yangtze or locating Wuhu on a map of China.

With Brownie, Dottie's mother, Mae Willis Brown, we struggled with spelling "demons," while Grandma Watters, Hyla Doc's mother, Ada Stowell Watters, who came to live with her when widowed, taught us to call by name the birds and wildflowers. Grandma Watters also taught us to locate the North Star; then with her lively telling of the ancient stories of beasts and men on starry nights when we lay on blankets out on the lawn, she turned the heavens into a near and friendly place.

The few other Wuhu foreign children came and went according to boarding school schedules. Most of them left home at the age of seven while I stayed, Mother willing to guide me through the Calvert System, which had been devised to prepare American children, isolated as I was, to enter American schools. I learned to find my own entertainments, to enjoy hours of solitude.

The rich, noisy, turbulent life beyond the compound wall inevitably drew me, while Hyla Doc and Grandma Watters unwittingly subsidized excursions into it by swelling my small supply of allowance coppers. En route to China Grandma Watters had met aboard ship a man whose mission it was to find a natural predator for the insect devouring Hawaii's pineapple crop. She sent him specimen insects, but enfeebled with Parkinson's Disease could not collect them herself so held "beetle hours" when I took to her new and strange bugs for which she paid a copper each. Hyla Doc also collected insects for the London School of Tropical Medicine and paid the same remarkable sum. I became a determined insect hunter.

This business venture made possible quick trips into the streets to bargain for water chestnuts or sesame candies or *pao-tzu*, the marvelous dough-wrapped vegetables with sometimes a bit of shrimp or pork, carried by vendors who would set down their carrying poles at the gatehouse and uncover their savory pots. I never grew tired of watching them lift and carry their tantalizing loads, once tried the knee-bent jog with pole across my shoulder, for which I got a laughing ovation from a quickly gathered crowd as I managed the feat without slopping.

At night, laced into the texture of those early years, the murmuring voices of my parents from their room next to mine, the drumming of rain on our corrugated iron roof along with the beat of their love, and my father's migraine groans subsiding toward sleep, were comforting sounds that settled finally into the serenity of his voice raised in prayer.

Always slow to drift into sleep, I listened to the solitary notes of an *erh-hu*, the two-stringed Chinese fiddle, that slipped across our wall from the huts among the willows and through the tall French windows of my bedroom open to the river. A voice raised in song, sometimes far into the night, the haunting liquid notes of a flute, the clang of the night watchman's gong, the creak of oars and muffled voices, a waft of gardenia from the hedge below or the pungent early morning fragrance from buckets of night soil collected for the fields: these were the assurances that all was well.

But to this day I can hear in my head the high thin wailing that meant another death. I always worried if it were a child, for children's graves were often too shallow. It was my self-imposed task to steal out to watch over a new grave and rebury fragments dug up during the night by dogs. My nails were always dirty, my chest a tight lump in my middle. An old coolie caught me once, digging a deeper grave. He scooped me up and took me away from there and set me down on a mound of sweet grasses behind the schoolhouse for children of hospital staff. There we shared a cigarette, passing it back and forth, my scold silent after his first tirade. I was comfortable with him, for I understood his outburst was provoked by concern, and I was comfortable because he was a coolie. Mother used to say that as an infant I would scream should a foreigner try to pick me up, but would go to any old beggar.

I have forgotten how it was we were discovered. Much was made of the fact that I was caught smoking, and my friend received a scolding in his turn. But he did not tell why it was we sat there together, and we exchanged a glance that told me it was a secret between us. I have not told it either, until now.

My Chinese life, as I moved beyond the protective walls of Ichishan, became more secretive as the gulf between the energetic foreign world and the brooding immensities that underlay our ancient city of Wuhu became more apparent to me. Born a bubbler, at first I overflowed with

12

tales of my small adventures, spilled out over lunch or supper, and was told not to be so imaginative. When I complained that my Chinese friends were cold and was told not to worry, that they were used to it, I was left with the cry of the young Chinese woman ringing in my head, "*Wo pa leng,*" I fear cold, and was puzzled. Slowly I learned to hold my tongue.

At home a brisk air was charged with words like grit. Gumption. Spunk. Count your blessings. If at first you don't succeed, try, try, again. The Lord helps those who help themselves. Out on the streets, ah, out on the streets there was time to stare, to stop whatever you were doing to watch a fight or listen to a screaming quarrel, to poke in the mud to see what underlay it, or to lie flat on your back among the water buffaloes grazing in the field and watch the clouds float by. The sense of being a small part within the massive flow of history that permeates Chinese painting and informs ordinary lives, creates a view of the world, a pace and place within it, that differ from those of the West where individuals take their lives in hand to shape them.

I puttered around the compound gate and wandered down Ta ma-lu, First Street, drawn to the city's presence, old and venerable and without any particular interest in me as it absorbed me, and would have sucked me under again as it has the spirits and gods and beasts and men it has tossed up and drawn under over the past two thousand five hundred years. Lying in the floodplain of the Yangtze that drains a thousand miles of runoff, and long known by other names, Wuhu, Reed Lake, was the name that washed over it five centuries before Christ as it steamed and stank and sank beneath recurring floods that left famine, cholera, typhoid and typhus in their wake. When the waters subsided, people still lived knee-deep in rice paddies, hacking their ways through chronic bronchitis and tuberculosis, picking at ulcers and learning to walk with gigantic tumors. Down the centuries into my life they drooped and dropped with schistosomiasis, while around them edged the blind and those with a leg or an eye or a hand missing, lepers with half-eaten away, puffy and pasty faces, listless opium smokers with vacant eyes.

Along with Anching further west along the Yangtze and Hofei the capital of Anhwei to the north, Wuhu on the south bank of the river is a leading town of a province that was, and is, hard to reach, poor, and less well known to foreigners than some others.

This was not always true. A commercial town since the Ming (1368-

1644), Wuhu for a short time shone as one of China's four great rice centers early in the Ch'ing (1644-1911). The city lies within the Chiangnan (south of the Yangtze) region, where rivers and canals provide good transportation for the wood, tea, paper, lacquer and ink sticks of southern Anhwei which were renowned throughout China during the Southern Sung (1127-1279). On them and later on rice and cotton as well, was based the rise of the famous Huichow merchants during the Ming. In the sixteenth century these merchants began to play a major role in China's economy, even to dominate it for a time as a change in government salt trade policies benefited them, and a circulating economy began to replace self-sufficient local commerce. As the merchants amassed wealth, they built luxurious homes and took concubines, supported drama groups and public works and enhanced their standing among the literati by collecting works of Anhwei painters. This in turn promoted an upsurge in the development of the spare yet diverse Anhwei painting style that commands attention again today.

With the decay of the Ming dynasty and conquest of the Manchus (1644), the glory of the Anhwei School went into decline along with the great merchants. During the Taiping Rebellion (1845-1864) armies fought over the province leaving whole cities uninhabited as people were killed or fled, and for years after, squatters venturing into empty houses found skeletons lying about. Gradually the province was repopulated, but since 1700 Anhwei has in general been bitterly poor.

Wuhu became a treaty port in 1876; what prosperity it knew was always linked to the Yangtze, the magnet that drew sampans and sailboats down hundreds of miles of streams and canals. By the time my parents reached the city in 1922, freighters on the river flew flags from all over the world, and Wuhu had become a center for electricity and telegraph service. Within another decade a motor road and then a slender rail line penetrated thickets of superstition, high land values and xenophobia to cross the rice fields, canals and grave mounds to link Wuhu with Nanking and Shanghai.

There were thirty to forty foreign families in Wuhu during the 1930s, the years I remember best: Jewish doctors exiled from Europe; Spanish Catholics; White Russian businessmen, elegant and tired; Protestant missionaries; diplomats of the British and Japanese consulates; personnel of the Salt Gabelle (staffed throughout China by many foreign officials, by the French in Wuhu) and of the Chinese Maritime Customs (whose commissioner was British); managers of the Asiatic Petroleum Company of London, of the American Standard Oil, of a Japanese cotton mill, of a German electric plant; and personnel of the large British East Asian shipping concerns, Jardine, Matheson and Co. and Butterfield and Swire.

It was an era of snowy linens and fingerbowls, when, except for close friends, the adults addressed one another as missus or mister, and single adults were aunts and uncles to us children. When we gathered at the Customs Club to set off Guy Fawkes Day fireworks, or at their respective consulates to celebrate birthdays of the reigning monarchs of Great Britain and Japan, it was a nineteenth century setting in which ladies were elegant in long gowns and elbow gloves, ships' officers resplendent in gold braid, cocked hats and ceremonial swords. At lawn and tennis parties, men in white shorts shouted "Good show!" and beamed good sportsmanship as they shook hands vigorously over the net, while the ladies saw to a procession of silent, long-robed house servants with trays of tall lemon drinks and tiny cucumber sandwiches to be consumed in languor under the willows lining the courts.

At the towering red brick convent and school of the Spanish Catholic mission, we other foreigners entered singly or in pairs and spoke quietly, Chinese our common language, the sisters twittering with excitement and slippering in and out with tea and cakes, always happy to have guests but never venturing to our homes in return.

For a time I was enrolled in their advertised class for French. My parents hoped I would be in a class of Chinese students, but I was the only one and often found my teacher bent over her harp in a dim fragrant chapel. More musician than teacher, Mother Auxilia forgot lessons while I stretched out on a hard bench to listen and emerged from her class with a limited Spanish-flavored French, now forgotten, but a lasting delight in the quiet of the convent and the loveliness of Mother Auxilia. It is only as I recall her that I realize she was gnarled with arthritis, a hunchback who moved with difficulty.

When a new British commissioner of customs arrived in Wuhu, a strained silence held between mission and business communities until my father suddenly realized that, as leader of the social scene, Mrs. Wilding, the Commissioner's wife, was waiting for calling cards to be left on the silver tray at her door. After that oversight was remedied, I was frequently invited to play with a daughter my age whose name I have forgotten, while never can I forget that of her brother, St. John (pronounced *sinjun*). When I stayed overnight he left the skull of a cat in my bath *kang* (a large round earthenware crock), distributed holly leaves under my bedsheets and shut into my room the only fierce one of nine Great Danes. The Wilding household was of great interest to me with its formal British manner and soda water to drink, a cross old poodle who lorded it over the larger dogs and two tigers caged at the back of the house. When an older daughter was home from boarding school, I followed her about entranced with her ability to sketch, the happy recipient of her cast-off pencil stubs and erasers.

Green Hill, Phoenix Hill, Lion Hill, Iron Hill, Go-around-rock Hill: Wuhu was dotted with mission compounds. Largely isolated from the mainstream of Chinese experience by walls, ours was a containment sought not only by foreigners in a land where missionaries were often regarded with hostility and knew from experience how quickly lives could be forfeit, how unprotected school and hospital supplies disappeared, but also a containment encouraged by Chinese officials who refused protection for unwalled properties and preferred to isolate Western influences.

Rooted deep within Chinese culture itself, the compound wall was a variation on the medieval city wall prevalent throughout Europe as well as China before weapons transcended walls, a variation of the stockade of our own frontier, even of the Chinese family home built around courtyards, with its back to the world to assure some measure of privacy and protection.

There was a constant seepage of missionaries into the larger Chinese world from behind those walls. I remember Aunt Bertha Cassidy, of the American Advent Missionary Society, bundled up in her padded gown to step into a junk for her regular inland trips up the streams that laced the countryside; my father putting on good walking shoes and disappearing across the rice paddies for days at a time to conduct the business of his vast district in its villages; Hyla Doc snatching up her black bag to head for rickshaw or launch in answer to a call for help.

Our hill was outside the walled city of Wuhu when my parents arrived there in 1922. Crowned by the Wuhu General Hospital, it was and is a landmark for Yangtze shipping. My life was at first centered in a huge old brick house, one of three on the slope toward the river built for foreign staff on Ichishan. These old houses sagged with years of damp and insects and neglect, but had wonderful high ceilings and large verandahs.

Ours stood closest to the road at the bottom of the hill, above Mother's vegetable and flower gardens that stretched to the wall topped with broken glass. Outside the wall a row of catalpas, showy with large lavender blooms in season, lined Ta ma-lu facing the huts among the willows behind the dike along the Yangtze. Originally built as a school but converted to house whoever was resident evangelist, ours became known as the Hayes House as we moved in and out of it, finally settling in as its more permanent residents.

Our kitchen was ell to a square, front door flanked by parlor on the left, my father's study on the right, dining room behind his study with a swing door to the kitchen. A center hall from the front door connected to the schoolroom, at the back at the foot of the stairway, which ran behind the parlor to French doors opening on the garden. Upstairs were four bedrooms, a bath and storeroom. Fireplaces in each of three rooms downstairs and two up were insufficient to warm this large house, so a coal-burning stove was set up in winter at the foot of the stairway, its stovepipe leading through a heating drum in the bathroom above.

There was some wicker furniture left behind by earlier missionaries, a large blue sofa with broken springs, an enormous wardrobe in each bedroom and a huge brass bed in mine. To furnish the house further, my father got out a Montgomery Ward catalogue as guide for sketches from which a Wuhu carpenter constructed his flattop desk and swivel chair, a round dining room table, chairs and side table, and some bedroom furniture.

There was nothing of value in the whole house, yet to the Chinese it represented a way of life steeped in riches unavailable to them. It was but slowly that I became aware of the banter over my head and was able to interpret it: "We had that book, let me see, was it in our second library or the third?" asked the Episcopal bishop of his wife, whose home had been looted more than once. "Guess where I found my dishes last week! Thought we'd never see them again but Brownie says I can have them back for what she paid at the thieves market," was another kind of remark. Discovering one's dishes or silver on a friend's table was a common experience, but more usual than theft was the borrowing back and forth that went on between servants.

My father's study, a large square room with windows opening out to the river, bookshelves lining the walls and his desk centered so that daylight poured over his shoulders, was my favorite room. Sometimes I

would sit for hours examining the array of family photographs or finger-
ing small daybooks he received as advertisements from oil companies
and banks and stacked near the floor for my benefit. Occasionally I mer-
ited one for my own. He was a stamp collector and invited me to help
soak stamps off envelopes, then dry them on his gooseneck desk lamp
while we poured over his atlas to find the countries from which they had
come. His bottom left drawer was emptied to become my own, and I
often sat on the floor near him busy with pencils and paper, soaking up
atmosphere and language while he worked with his Chinese secre-
tary/teacher or murmured aloud to himself as he prepared sermons and
reports. When the barber made his monthly visits, it was in the study
that the large dictionary was placed on my father's chair and I reluctantly
on it, for the Dutch bob left me a shorn, plain child, unlike my attractive
mother.

In the dining room opening off his study through double doors, we
had Western breakfasts (orange juice, Postum for my parents, toast and
shredded wheat, sometimes a boiled egg) made exciting by the daily appearance of the hospital shopper who would add to his list items our
cook would not purchase. When I had enough coppers, I could add my
order for a small ruled notebook. Lunches were Chinese, often in the
hospital dining room, dinners usually Western.

There were seldom fewer than eight or a dozen gathered around our
table, and we could see the river while we ate, could easily keep track of
the steamers making the Yangtze run between Shanghai and Hankow,
most of them carrying passengers who came to stay for a night or a week,
or a year: lecturers and evangelists from America, England or Europe,
specialists surveying flood or epidemic, medical students come to Wuhu
Hospital for special training, refugee missionaries from disturbed areas.
These people of different backgrounds, different ways of thinking, with
news from interior China or America or Europe or India or Korea, gave a
proportion to our lives of which I was unaware until we reached America
where our outlook was far more provincial.

In the dining room a sideboard housed the marshmallows and saltines that could be found only in Shanghai, strictly-rationed treats available only through the once-a-month order. Shortly before we left China
an icebox was added in one corner, making it possible for us to have cold
watermelon and for Mother to experiment in making ice cream. Fruits
like watermelon had to be cleaned off before we cut into them, with alco-

hol that was sometimes set alight. I never knew until we reached America that bananas were yellow. Until the advent of the icebox, spoilage was delayed by placing food in a wind cupboard, a wooden box, its sides covered with screening, that was suspended outside the kitchen door on the shady side of the house. But most perishables were purchased daily. Sweets attracting insects were stored in a small cupboard on spindly legs set into cans of kerosene.

It was in the dining room that I had to stand patiently while the tailor measured me for a new dress; where the shoemaker traced my growing feet on brown wrapping paper for the shoes that always hurt.

It was in the dining room after breakfast that Mother sat down with our cook each day to figure accounts, plan meals and work assignments. Chang Shih-fu (master workman, or cook, Chang) presided not only over the kitchen but also over the other servants. The Chinese expected all foreigners to provide employment for servants at wages considerably more than they could earn elsewhere, and we had four, the number old-timers recommended. Our gardener was Hsiao Chang (young Chang), a strong young man and tall, who helped me plant my own garden. He was usually hard at work digging or weeding or off on mysterious errands of his own.

Lao Ma (old Ma) our "boy," who looked to be a hundred years old but was actually younger than my father, sighed and ached and watered Mother's paper flowers and dusted her real ones and retreated into his miseries. He also mopped floors, washed clothes using a scrub board, and before the new hospital was built and telephones linked the foreign houses, he also kept everyone in touch by carrying chits from one to another.

Chu Sao-tzu (older brother's wife, or auntie, Chu), my sister's amah, tended bedrooms and bath, and did the fine ironing. Taciturn and jealous of the baby, she drove me away from the laughing golden-curled infant, more than eight years younger than I, with a tight-lipped anger so that it was not until we and our children were grown that my sister, Lois Anne, and I came to know and enjoy each other.

Mornings started early, especially during the hot season. Chang Shih-fu, back from market to start the charcoal fire for lunch in the Chinese brick stove, would collect water needed for cooking. Until the new hospital was built, when cold water was piped into our home by gravity from holding tanks on the hospital roof, all our water was carried from the river by coolies who jogged out through the Water Gate at the end of our garden, and clambered down the slick stone steps built into the river bank to scoop up the dirty yellow liquid which they dumped into a filtration system beside our kitchen door. This was a wooden structure of three levels with a large earthenware *kang* on each level filled with alternate layers of sand, charcoal and palm fibers. As the water flowed down through these crocks, each probably thirty-six inches wide and twenty-eight high, the water came out fairly clear and could be used for scrubbing and laundry. But for cooking and drinking, it was then poured into a galvanized filter in which it passed through further layers of purifying cotton, then boiled for twenty minutes.

Black hair standing straight up in surprise over black eyes that darted back and forth (with ocular nystagmus, Hyla Doc told me recently, when all those years I thought it was his special laughter) Chang Shih-fu, our cook, let me grind peanuts for the soup that stuck to the roofs of our mouths, and asked why it was we always smelled our soup with eyes shut before tasting it. I would look up from prayers to see his face framed in the window of the swing door to the kitchen, his puzzled eyes darting back and forth.

My best friend, my willing collaborator, Chang Shih-fu set aside for me bits of tofu or peanuts, a bowl of *feng-tzu*, mung bean noodles, which he knew I loved and made up a rhyme about using my name. He gave me packets of *pao-tzu* to sustain pretended safaris into darkest Africa with my friend Dottie.

One time when Chang Shih-fu fetched me from a sleep-over at the customs compound, I didn't want to go home and led him on a chase: hiding in bamboo groves, under shrubs, behind sheds. Finally, along a driveway where he caught me, I grabbed his hat and tossed it over a hedge onto what I thought was grass. To my horror it teetered, then slowly sank through the scum of a pond, taking my bravura with it. My good friend, his eyes wildly darting, plunked me into a rickshaw and walked along beside me the entire way home, shouting aloud my misdeeds to an amused public. He repeated the story, with embellishments and relish, to my father, for which I received my severest spanking. Later, in the kitchen, he was grim-faced as he chopped vegetables with extra vigor while I sidled up and stood beside him without speaking. Then he reached down the end of a carrot with a sidelong glance, and seeing I held nothing against him laughed with me, his eyes twinkling with more than the disease as we went on as before.

Chang Shih-fu carved for me two swords out of wood, their blades sanded to fine edges and curved to points, with handles that fit my small hand, elegant carvings with a heft that gave special pleasure. They were among my treasures packed away in the attic when we left Wuhu, and I have regretted that I did not think to give them to Hsiao Pao and Hsiao Shih. In games of warlord with the boys I was always disappointed to have to surrender the swords to them, while I got tied to the enormous trunk of an old wisteria and suffered the fate of the unfortunate missionary.

Most constant among friends near my age, Hsiao Pao and Hsiao Shih came over the wall with my help. It was topped with broken bits of glass cemented into wicked but beautiful teeth that sparkled in sun and moonlight, and was edged within the compound by a hedge of yucca spikes. The first time they whistled I carefully cleared out a clump of yucca so that I could reach the top of the wall, closer to the ground within the compound at that spot than from the road, and smashed down the glittering glass teeth on top. We stood around not knowing what to say, so they taught me to kick a coin with chicken feathers tied through its square hole. The object of shuttlecock is to keep the bird, the "kicker," in the air as long as possible, with the side of the heel. Experts get pretty fancy, kicking it behind the back, or back and forth to a partner, and Hsiao Pao was an expert.

After that, whenever the boys were free of their grueling routines in the fields, we fished or caught turtles in the duck pond, shot marbles in the dust or scavenged the hospital dump. We swung in the heavy wisteria vines, climbed the tall photinia, collected mulberry leaves for my silk worms, cut up old oiled-paper umbrellas to make slingshots, leaving two ribs for handles and a stretch of oiled paper between into which we could fit a smooth, round stone.

Hsiao Pao had a round pocked face, Hsiao Shih a thin one. Hsiao Pao talked and smiled a lot and always beat me at shuttlecock with panache followed by some comforting remark like how much better I was at climbing trees. Hsiao Shih seemed a little older, more uneasy to be inside the compound, and he took my marbles with triumph. After a while I followed them outside the wall.

When the water buffaloes lazily turned homeward, leaving the meadow behind the huts among the willows in the late afternoons, the two boys liked to run up bright kites against a wind toward a sky reaching to lift them. One was a red butterfly that they showed me how to launch, how to hold the roller, feet braced against the tug of the sky creature on its reins, then race against the wind as it soared. They soon wound it down and took me along into the huts where their mothers strained over tiny stitches in the smoky gloom, dragons and fishes and birds taking shape on red and blue slippers under fingers that by day cracked stones for the new roadbed.

Hsiao Pao's mother was round and comfortable as he was, her face also pocked and pitted, her eyes a welcoming brown as she showed me her work and told stories of kind goddess Kuan-yin. Hsiao Pao's mother, a leaner version of him and as distant, threw chatter over her shoulder, stories of the *hu-li*, the fox-spirits that would catch me for wandering off from my home and causing her trouble. Her black eyes snapped and stood me against the mud wall and did not invite me to lean against the warm clay stove. But as I became a more constant visitor and nothing harmful happened, she took less notice of me. More of our games took place in the dooryards among the chickens and pigs and the infants with flies clustered around their eyes and snot running down from their noses.

When blinding clouds of locusts blanketed the countryside and camera crews appeared to film background scenes for the movie of Pearl Buck's novel, *The Good Earth*, we collected the huge insects to feed our turtles in the now unused filtration *kang*. When the locusts swarmed and left, it was a stripped and strangely silent countryside, a hungry year they left behind.

After the buffalo ambled home from the meadow behind the huts in the late afternoons, and the old men took in their birdcages after sunning their prized thrushes, and the young men brought out their cages of fighting crickets, and the boys rolled down their kites, we helped gather up buffalo dung, sweet with the aroma of grass, and slapped it moist against the sides of the huts to dry for winter fuel.

As we walked along Ta ma-lu the beggars (who would be clawing about me with their disfigured hands begging coppers the instant I was in a rickshaw) lay listless, sometimes repairing the wax makeup that created their most gruesome afflictions, ignoring me as they knew there was nothing in my pockets. Down by the ponds we watched fishermen tie strings around the necks of their fishing cormorants, while in the spring I watched the two boys help plant, then transplant, rice, wading through paddies bent over to place, one by one, each seedling. They came out of the paddies with faces scorched from sun reflecting off the water, bare legs festooned with leeches that they peeled off, then straightened tired backs. Usually too tired to chatter, once they excitedly told how they had caught and killed a Yangtze crocodile that had dug into the bank of the paddy.

When the camel caravans came down from the northwest, we ran to the roadside to watch them march along, their humps ragged in the heat, heads high in a disdain that matched that of the men and women with big easy feet, finely embroidered tunics in bright colors, round, colorful caps on their shining black hair, so in contrast to the blues, greys and blacks of our area. We wondered who they were and where they came from and where they were going, and the boys shouted their questions but got no answers.

From the rickshaw pullers, inveterate smokers, we begged empty matchboxes with pictures of tigers and ladies glued to their lids. After funeral processions we picked out of the dirt spirit money strewn along the way to ward off ghosts. Some was always saved to be burnt with other paper offerings at the grave to assure the dead comfort in their new world.

During the great flood of 1931, Hsiao Pao's father rowed us down Ta ma-lu. When a strong current threatened to sweep us out into the river, he leaned back "to get right with myself," as he got a fix on the direction in which we were being carried and lined up the bow of the sampan with a point on Ichishan.

We stood side by side in 1932 when the Japanese flagship *Idzuwo* rounded the bend in the river at the head of a flotilla sent on patrol in a show of strength. From the silent fury of my friends I acquired a prejudice against all that is Japanese, strengthened by what happened when they took Nanking and then Wuhu some years later. It is a prejudice that lingers.

Sometimes when I went into the huts a bowl of *mien* or cabbage was set in front of me, while at New Year I was given chopsticks and urged to share *chiao-tzu*. During the Dragon Boat Festival *tsung-tzu*, sticky rice balls in lotus leaves, were pressed on me, and I began to feel uncomfortable eating their food when they had so little. I went less often into the huts, mostly to hear Pao Mama's tales of O Mi To Fu, the great god of all with arms outstretched in protection; of Yünlo (he seemed to me kindly, but I have been told he was ferocious) who stood at the gates of hell and escorted lost souls to the depths to match their misdeeds; of Ti Ts'ang the redeemer, who refused Buddhahood and reported to Yünlo for service and was sent to help the lost repent. My favorite was Kuan-yin, the Goddess of Mercy, who also refused Buddhahood to stay where she might be of help to suffering humans.

There was an ancient rhythm in the Chinese countryside, in the threshing of rice from its hulls on the hard-baked mud courtyards, in the chop that came from bamboo groves being harvested for the thousand-and-one daily utensils used throughout China. There it was, half a mile down Ta ma-lu from Ichishan, at the local government office as we watched the tile roof of the *yamen* being replaced, repeated in the graceful throw and catch of each handful of gray tiles from the man on the ground to the man on the roof, who would turn in tempo and place them in alternating rows curved upwards and down so as to keep the roof watertight.

The beat had sounded for centuries in the dip of oar or sweep on sampan and junk, in the dip and ladle of night soil from buckets to manure *kang* along the fields, in the slap of wooden paddles on laundry dipped in the pond and on flat rocks pounded, without soap, into cleanliness. It matched the tread of the buffalo hitched to water lifts to irrigate the fields and the squeal of wood within wood of the round pin that centered these wheels. Elsewhere men stood all day treading wooden water pumps, their arms hooked over a pole to ease their weight, a rice-straw thatch shading them from the sun.

What a watery world it was of streams, canals, rivers, ponds, lakes, high humidity, an average yearly rainfall of upwards of fifty inches, and of floods; a wet world in which it was difficult to come by safe drinking water. I never fully dried out until we reached America, and among life's strange paradoxes I count the assuaging of thirst that came with the harsh break from my muted wet world into the brisk driven West.

The Yangtze was a strong presence in our lives, our highway inland and to the coast, and an ever-changing pageant in itself. It was a medieval world we lived in, and it was only shortly before we left China that a motor road and rail line were built. Airmail service between Shanghai and Hankow, with a brief stop at Wuhu, predated both road and rail.

My world may have been a child's, but I heard names over my head and made some tangled sense of them: Chiang Kai-shek, Mao Tse-tung, Chu Teh, Wu P'ei-fu, Chang Tso-lin, Wang Ching-wei. I could see people about me who dressed in rags, whose teeth were broken, black or missing, who tore bark off trees to eat in famine years, who stumbled and fell and did not get up. I wondered why I lived in a large clean house and slept between clean white sheets and ate my dinner at a table set with a crisp white cloth. When I played with Hsiao Pao and Hsiao Shih, I wore my oldest clothes, my blue cloth sandals.

OUR COMPOUND, Ichishan, with an elbow of rock that jutted perilously into the river for the great junks, was a pleasantly wooded five acres, the back of the hill an ancient graveyard seldom visited except when I roamed there picking wild flowers. Once I fell through the rotting boards of a coffin into a pile of ribs, where I sat for a time sorting out bones and mulling over the contrast of their dry brittleness with the remains in new graves; then I covered it and left it in peace.

Wuhu Hospital crested the hill, its approach a narrow dike between rice paddies until the new hospital was built in 1927. Then the dike was widened into Ta ma-lu, First Street, or literally Big Horse Street, for it was wide enough for a horse and carriage.

A dozen or more rickshaw pullers gathered daily at the gatehouse, hopeful for business as they spent their days smoking, gossiping and rinsing off mud that had collected on rickshaw wheels and spattered the yellow *yu-pu,* the oiled cloth that could be drawn up in front of the passenger and hooked in place as protection against rain. They squatted in the dirt with their gambling sticks or bowls of cabbage and *mien,* the noodles made in the long mud hut factory down the road, and exchanged news with passing vendors and the soldiers with fixed bayonets stationed each side of the gate.

The hospital rickshaw, used by Hyla Doc to reach T'ieh Fang-tzu, the "iron house" clinic in the city, built of corrugated iron to forestall deterioration, was a gleaming black lacquer and sported shiny oil lamps hung on each side for night travel, a cut above the public red-brown rickshaws that drooped with a weariness to match that of their pullers. When Dottie's father, Robert Brown, shipped his Ford from America, there were few Wuhu streets wide enough for it to travel, but it stood in the gateway polished daily to a shiny readiness, a readiness that sprang to life when the Japanese bombed the city in 1937 and it went forth to gather up the wounded.

Within the gate a winding road led to the hospital at the top of the hill, passed houses for nurses and maintenance staffs, workshops, gardens and tennis court, a primary school for staff children, and the three old houses for foreign staff, Hyla Doc's, the Browns' and ours.

About two hundred people lived on Ichishan, about a dozen of us foreigners. As my life moved outward from our house it began to revolve around the hospital, where we went for typhoid and cholera shots and smallpox vaccinations; where my sister was born and Hyla Doc operated on Mother for appendicitis; where my father, superintendent while Robert Brown was on furlough, carried me after I broke one thing or another; where doctors from British and American warships came to help out and to brush up on their surgical skills; where I counted the bones on Sally, the skeleton in the nurses' classroom, and loved to startle visitors by whisking off the drape that hid her.

Hyla Doc, barely five feet tall, blond waves cropped to be easily stuffed under her white surgery cap, operated while standing on a stool. Noting my interest in all that went on, she issued me cap, gown and mask and had me hold x-rays for her in surgery. I remember her staggering off that stool, arms clasped around a $64\frac{1}{2}$ pound tumor, chuckling, "A tumor on the table is worth two in the tummy!" Preserved, it became an object of awe, another favorite stop on my tour for visitors. The patient, a thirty-year-old woman, had been carried on a bamboo bed by members of her family for four days and four nights after neighbors raised enough money to make the journey possible. She had to learn to walk again after losing her unusual weight.

Friends among the nurses gave me small jobs to do (empty bedpans, mop up spills) while Frances Culley, Superintendent of Nurses, her dark eyes snapping, set about teaching me how to change a dressing. Seeing in me a likely candidate for nursing school, she had a miniature student nurse uniform made for me one Christmas. I played with young patients well enough to play, sang with others and made "rounds" to see older patients with whom I enjoyed talking. I begged empty bottles from Aunt Culley and Hyla Doc. I visited Lao Wang, the engineer, with whom I liked to sit in comfortable silence in the engine room where we could feel that mechanical heart at work pumping water, lighting the compound, creating current for X-ray, for boiling water and heating steam kettles for the laundry, and for running the elevator.

The emotional climate on the hill often fluctuated with the progress or decline of special patients. On my "rounds" I stopped to play with Pollyanna, a loving, trusting five-year-old brought in one night breathing with difficulty after sucking a melon seed into her larynx at a wedding party. She survived the tracheotomy and operation to remove the seed and returned to her naturally merry self, often visiting us after she recovered. Another happy youngster, Hsiao Mei, Little Sister, had been sold as a small child by her poor family to a theatrical woman to be trained in stunts or as a serving girl. Her owner was not about to spend money on her, so she lacked food and clothing, and one winter her feet froze, gangrene set in and one foot dropped off before she was brought to the hospital. Emaciated, fearful, Hsiao Mei had to have both lower legs amputated. But during recovery she responded to food, warmth and care, becoming a rosy, cheerful child always demanding, "Give me my shoes!" and jumping around with her stumps thrust into them. Money for artificial legs was found and she was lodged in a home for cripples where she received care and training to support herself.

Hsiao Hu, Little Tiger, was one of the most frightening patients I remember. An eleven-year-old country boy, he had suffered a bladder stone since the age of five, literally writhing in pain for several years before being brought for help. On admission he rolled on the floor biting his own flesh and biting and scratching anyone who came near him. The stone was retrieved, and while it took a long time before he stopped biting and scratching, his pain-lined face, which made him look like a little old man, broke into smiles after surgery.

The foreigners among whom I lived had better houses than my Chinese friends, they walked differently, ate different foods, spoke different languages, told different tales, worshipped different gods. The names Beebe, Stuart, Maddock, Gaunt drifted vaguely by me, as I hung around listening to the adults talk, while Aunt Bertha Cassidy, who had spent her own childhood in Wuhu, told how Our Dear Dr. Hart had placed handholds with chains strung between them along the rocks beneath our house so that trackers hauling huge junks upriver could keep from being dragged off into the current. Uncle Joe Wharton of the Christian Missionary Alliance, showed me a headstone in our cemetery cut with the name Edgerton Hart. He took a cutting of the yellow rose that bloomed beside it and planted it by Hyla Doc's porch.

Who were all these people? Was I one of them? Why were we so different from the Chinese? Why did we live on Ichishan? What was the story into which I had been born? Although I had a distinct sense of being some small part of a larger flow of life, I had no sense of connection with the Pilgrims studied with Mother, and it was clear the stories that were so much a part of my Chinese friends had no part in the lives of my parents. Rumors of wars floated over my head and I was vaguely aware Hyla Doc had a stream of battle casualties to patch up, but I had no inkling of the tumultuous history through which Wuhu Hospital had survived to reach those few years of relative calm, nor of the grim years it faced ahead.

TWO HUNDRED FIFTY YEARS behind the first European Catholics, Protestants began their work in Canton in the 1800s, but my parents' church, the Methodist, was the last of the great Protestant denominations to send missionaries to China.

Moses and Isabel White and Judson Collins stepped out of their chartered lorcha anchored near the Foochow Customs House in 1837. They had left Boston four months earlier, sailing around the Cape of Good Hope and across the Pacific to Hong Kong where they were delayed by illness and weather another two weeks before they could start up the Min River.

Delay. Illness. Weather. These would be a constant backdrop to struggles with language, with difficulties in finding and maintaining places in which to live, teach and preach, to Chinese indifference, harassment and active opposition. They did not know that Isabel White would succumb to the inhospitable climate within the year, nor that it would take ten years of work before their mission could claim a convert. "We are unable to report favorably of this mission," read the annual report for 1853, "it seems to have suffered from. . . adverse causes. . . ."

Anti-foreign riots. Revolution. Disturbances, troubles or unsettled times in mission parlance: these were to be a perennial part of China missions for the next hundred years. Yet the work began to spread, and the optimistic vision was of a belt of Christian influence some three hundred miles wide, stretching through central China from its eastern seaboard to Tibet.

This grand view was not to be realized, but Kiukiang, centrally located on the Yangtze at the foot of Lushan about five hundred miles west of Shanghai, became a focus for mission work. It was a gateway to Kiangsi to its south, Hubei to its north and Anhwei eastward.

Sailing up the Yangtze in 1867 to start Methodist work in Kiukiang,

Vergil C. Hart caught sight of the commanding bluff that was Ichishan when his junk passed Wuhu. The contrast of the great rock that had to be circumnavigated by all upriver traffic, with the flat, steamy rice paddies, rape and mustard fields to the south of the river and the wheat fields stretched away to the north, brought Hart to his feet. As this distinguished gentleman, strikingly erect and with a full walrus mustache, stood up to watch the hill disappear behind a bend in the river, he recognized the best site he had seen, one that could keep the feet of a mission out of water and create a haven for refugees. He resolved to return. This he did, and land was bought at Wuhu by the Methodist Mission in 1881.

Early work of a James Jackson and a Mr. Woodall, hazy figures in Methodist records, had disappeared when Robert C. Beebe was assigned to Wuhu in 1885 while he awaited completion of the Nanking Hospital to which he gave thirty years of distinguished service. He kept a small dispensary open during 1886, a year when high prices for food in China combined with tales of outrage against Chinese in America touched off riots in some Chinese cities in which mission properties were damaged and looted and missionaries spat upon and stoned.

When Dr. Beebe left for Nanking in 1887, George A. Stuart, physician, teacher, evangelist, editor and translator, another pioneer name in Methodist China mission history, was persuaded to turn aside from language study to keep the Wuhu clinic going.

"I am without medicines or anything to work with, and have no money to buy. I hope some friend will give us a start here immediately," Dr. Stuart wrote as he turned patients away. His was a plea to be echoed almost daily by doctors who followed him, their letters to the Board of Foreign Missions in New York always courteous, often desperate, their handwriting betraying the stress under which they worked. Throughout the history of China missions, needs far outstripped resources of all the mission boards combined.

Drugs for immediate use and funds enough to build a small hospital came in response to Dr. Stuart's plea, and by 1888 he was also running three outlying clinics for farmers with diseases of the eye, digestive tract and skin. He soon realized that Western medicine was making no reputation for the cure of any malady "unless perchance it may be worms or Itch," and that while dispensary work was useful as a means of meeting people it was valueless medically, even an "injury to the advance of foreign medicine" because of the impossibility of effecting cures for people who arrived too late to be treated or chose to follow their own ideas about taking medicine.

The hospital was built and patients moved in 1 October 1889. It consisted of one large building with wards for about forty patients, although ninety could be crowded in and usually were; operating and supply rooms; a cookhouse and two small buildings to house assistants, students and servants.

By 1896, when Edgerton Hart, Vergil Hart's son, was appointed to Wuhu Hospital, it was already a dilapidated wooden structure with two wards for men and one for women, lit by kerosene lamps hung from the ceilings. Patients provided their own clothing, bedding and food, and were cared for by family members who slept on the floor among chickens tied to the bedposts. Entire families were present at operations, where everything had to be explained to them.

Patients arrived at the foot of the hill and were carried by stretcher to an open porch, cold in winter, hot and filled with flies in summer, that served as an examining room. The admission bath was a portable wooden tub heated by a Chinese stove set into the wall and fired by reeds. It also heated the operating room sterilizer. Water arrived on two feet, carried in buckets slung from shoulder carrying poles and delivered from the river by a continuous line of coolies.

This was the hospital in which Edgerton Hart worked for seventeen years. This was the hospital that defeated nine doctors following him and sorely tried those who stayed with it. In spite of some improvements Edgerton Hart was able to make, this was Wuhu Hospital in 1922 when my parents arrived.

Our Dear Dr. Hart, who had so wanted to make Wuhu Hospital second to none in China, had to run dispensaries and earn funds to keep the hospital going by treating customs and consular families, and those of business representatives. There was no trained nurse to help with the women's work, no private rooms for Chinese of means who wanted and could pay for them, no facilities to lodge or treat opium addicts, whom he had to turn away.

In poor health himself, his wife and one of his seven children seriously ill, Dr. Hart was furloughed in 1899 only to return to find China reeling from the Boxer troubles and 48,000 square miles of Anhwei under water. Thirty million refugees faced famine and cholera, while the mission homes and hospital had badly deteriorated and suffered from thefts of five hundred dollars' worth of instruments, drugs and bedding.

Three years later Edgerton Hart wrote grimly, "We are a laughing stock. I wish you could see the state our hospital is in. . . . People on the floors . . . have walked and wheelbarrowed and taken sampans hundreds of miles to be treated." There was still no one to relieve him for even a day, and his own health began to break, and that of his wife, who fought a losing battle and died. By 1906 local gifts he had solicited from the Wuhu business community made possible some major repairs, and Caroline E. Maddock arrived as nurse. She was enthusiastic about increased accommodations for patients, a new laundry, the dark, sooty kitchen with earth floor replaced by a cement-floored room with large windows. Next to it another large sunny room was for dining and reading for ambulatory patients. Water was piped inside, powered by a windmill, another building erected for baths and barbering, clothing and oil storage, and a home was built for the senior physician, Dr. Chung, who was respected all over the countryside for his skills and character. No one would have blamed him had he accepted the invitation of Viceroy Chu Fu to build and take charge of a hospital in Nanking, a position that would have brought him rank, dear to Chinese hearts, and five times his Wuhu salary. But Dr. Chung chose to stay.

In 1906 Dr. Hart also petitioned the Mission Board for money to wall the compound, now enlarged to cover the hill, which was only partially fenced with bamboo. Theft was a big problem: instruments constantly stolen from the operating room, cash from the dispensary cash box, clothing from patients and staff. Work on a concession building down river (probably the American Standard Oil) brought many more strangers past the hospital, and no protection could be claimed from Chinese officials for unwalled property.

In the autumn of 1906 Edgerton Hart and Caroline Maddock were married. Things were looking up and ran relatively smoothly until the night of 4 June 1908, when part of the new hospital roof was torn away in a storm, an outbuilding was completely unroofed, walls caved in. The Mission Finance Committee made a special grant and work was started over.

By 1910 Dr. Hart was uncertain, not only about his beloved hospital, which seemed to deteriorate faster than he could keep it in repair and badly needed another doctor and a school of nursing for women, but was uncertain about his own life. "Perhaps I should seek employment," he wrote, "where I will be able to obtain enough income to meet living expenses and at the same time give my children an education. . . . My life has been given to and for Missions. I would like to remain in it."

Remain he did, with no doctor to relieve him, but 1913 was to best him. That the forty-eight-year-old physician was in failing health was apparent to friends who urged rest. When he picked up typhus from some refugees, in four days he was gone.

In 1926 Robert Brown recalled how Dr. Hart had made the Wuhu Hospital known throughout the Yangtze Valley: "His loving heart won the admiration of both the Chinese and the foreigners. The crews of half a hundred steamers that made the Yangtze run knew him and still speak of him."

Frank P. Gaunt reached Wuhu in 1915, Walter E. Libby in 1916, Robert E. Brown in 1917, Hyla S. Watters in 1925. Although Walter Libby was assigned to Nanchang after my parents' arrival in 1922, these were the doctors who stayed, and much of the prestige of the hospital that had slipped away after Dr. Hart's death was restored.

In 1918 the Wuhu School of Nursing was registered in time to provide extra hands to help with the 1919 cholera epidemic. The Chinese Red Cross asked the hospital to open a cholera hospital in the city, and for five weeks Walter Libby, two Chinese doctors and six student nurses ran the two hospitals and a dispensary. They walked into the city each day along streets lined with idols, often jammed with processions on which thousands of dollars had been spent to drive off the evil spirits causing the cholera. Priests and local doctors circulated stories that the foreigner was sucking the blood and cutting out the nerves of patients, but there was no violence, and as the epidemic brought foreigners and city officials into frequent contact, Chinese ideas of medicine began to change. Some wealthy people even began to complain that the hospital did not have rooms good enough for them. "For Chinese respect," wrote Dr. Libby, "we must give them the best and not belittle the Christian message."

Soon after my parents' arrival, a record keeper, librarian and administrative correspondent were appointed, kept full and accurate records and relieved the doctors of paper work. Then in 1923 the hospital, somewhat the worse for termites, rot, flood, famines, epidemics, rebellions and typhoons, burned down while Frank Gaunt moved his foreign patient under anesthesia to the outdoors and completed abdominal surgery. The Chinese fire department, aided by hospital staff and British bluejackets, fought the blaze and saved most of the drugs and other supplies, the library and records, and the Women's Annex. Fifty patients were evacuated to safety, bricks from the burned building were set aside for future use, and the hospital continued in a primitive building hastily thrown up at the foot of the hill. The Women's Annex was known as The Ark because it rode the hilltop. Its roof leaked so that Hyla Doc employed a coolie to hold an umbrella over her while delivering babies, and it was filled with smoke from the kitchen on its first floor, which also provided what heat there was. Surgical patients were carried by stretcher down the hill in all sorts of weather to the improvised surgery until finally a mud hut was built nearby for the women.

A visiting bishop in 1925 reported, "The Hospital consists of three parts—a magnificent site, a hole in the ground and an old shack where about 1,000 patients are being treated each month. This is the greatest opportunity for medical missionary work I have seen in China."

Controversies surrounded the building of the new hospital in which two strong-willed men were involved. Frank Gaunt was superintendent when Robert Brown arrived, and it was Gaunt's vision and initiative that brought the hospital into being. He is remembered as an able, intelligent and dedicated man, well-liked by his patients and those who did not have to work with or under him. But he seems to have been possessed by a high-handedness that damaged those who did, and it became clear to the bishop, L.J. Birney, that he must be returned to America and Robert Brown assigned the task to complete the building.

With some modifications, Frank Gaunt's plans were completed under Robert Brown's energetic and intelligent leadership in 1926-1927, during the period of unrest as Chiang Kai-shek set forth on his Northern Expedition. Although the project was not freed from conflicts over money, although Robert Brown fell sick, lost perspective in his fatigue, and neared despair, he persisted. He wrote the Board of Foreign Missions of his months of illness, fearful that if he broke down completely he couldn't support his family, of Brownie near exhaustion and Hyla Doc on the edge of her strength all winter and spring as she carried the medical work while he dealt with the construction problems. He went on to suggest that if they were to recall conditions in America during the influenza epidemic following the First World War when doctors and nurses could hardly get enough sleep to keep going, and realize that those were the conditions under which Wuhu doctors worked year-round, they could imagine the situation.

A cholera epidemic following occupation of Ichishan by Chiang's troops compounded problems and exhaustion, but the new hospital slowly took shape under the able direction of an Irish-American ex-marine named McGarin and his friend Chen, a former pirate who had a large price on his head when he appealed to McGarin for help. Chen went to work as his assistant when McGarin vouched for him with Chinese authorities and secured their grudging approval. In Wuhu Chen married a local girl, and when McGarin left, Chen stayed on to become one of the people most trusted and respected. He worked in the engineering room and drove the hospital car, and having had professional experience in opening locks without keys, was much in demand.

The central feature of the new hospital was a modern building equipped to care for one hundred patients and to provide for a school of nursing. On 8 December 1927 fire was made in the new boiler and the wards and halls were heated, as doors opened to the public. A brick building, with a stately portico of white columns at the entrance, it rose three stories in front and seven in the rear to conform to the hillside. On either side of the front steps sweeping up to the door over the ambulance entrance, were bronze plaques reading in Chinese, "Who is my neighbor?" and, "Not to be ministered unto but to minister." Hyla Doc suggested a round window over the front entrance, "Hyla's porthole," as we called it.

Western architecture was chosen because modern Chinese government and businesses were adopting Western style, but it was a simple, colonial design with a flat roof for patients to enjoy the sun and the sweeping view of town and countryside. A proud, gleaming, efficient plant designed by McKim, Mead & White, Wuhu Hospital was the equal of any in the United States. This is the hospital that stands on the banks of the Yangtze today.

Our dear Dr. Edgerton Hart, the sole physician and surgeon at Wuhu 1896-1913, gave his life for the people of Wuhu. In 1926 Dr. Brown wrote of his loving heart and the esteem in which Chinese and foreigners alike still held him.

Courtesy General Commission on Archives and History, The United Methodist Church

Paul G. Hayes

Known in our time as the Hayes House, this former school was shared with many visitors. It was occupied by Japanese soldiers during the 1937-1945 war. Although it is now a "condemned" house, several families live in it. The bamboo grove on the hillside is gone, a cement building occupies the yard, but the *kuei hua* tree, visible here, now stretches to the rooftop.

Wuhu General Hospital, built in 1889, burned down in 1923 while Dr. Frank Gaunt was operating. To the left is the Yangtze. The road, Ta ma-lu, led to the compound gate, around the hill and along the river. Flanked by rice paddies and mud huts when we lived there, the area has been engulfed by the city. A shipyard on the river extends across the old road, through the wall and garden to the foot of our home.

Looking from Ichishan toward the city in the 1890s, the Episcopal school stands out on Lion's Hill. Beyond it rises the cotton factory stack. The school is a vigorous school today and the factory has increased in size and productivity and is but one of a number of enterprises in this more modern city.

Both photos courtesy General Commission on Archives and History, The United Methodist Church.

Lebzelter's Donkey

IN THE TIME BEFORE I WAS BORN
WHO WAS IT WHO MADE ME SPROUT?

— WANG CHI (590-644)

In my memory my father strides across the yellow-brown landscape down Ta ma-lu in Wuhu, a short, spare man dressed all in white from pith helmet to buck shoes, green sleeve garters holding up his long white shirt sleeves, black umbrella and black New Testament in hand as he sets out to visit country churches. He is preceded by a coolie with a bamboo pole slung across his shoulders from which jounce a bedding roll and a small black suitcase for mission records and underwear. From such trips my father returned days later reddened by sun, browned by mud, his beard grown out and white.

I see him in the pulpit of the mission hospital chapel, his black-garbed figure tensed in entreaty, his eyes afire with inner vision, his whole frame reaching forward to gather into his embrace those who had never or seldom heard the Jesus story.

Sometimes, when I remember how the sound of his typewriter prompted me to crawl out of bed and sneak downstairs to watch him bent over his desk, his white, intense face emerging from the blackness above a small gooseneck lamp, utterly remote, concentrated, I see a man in lonely absorption continuing to wrestle free of the rigidities that shaped his youth, the attitudes so vigorously challenged by his seminary professors that he was shocked into new growth, growth that did not stop. Even in recent years he stopped dogmatic speakers with his, "Wait a moment!" and opened up new aspects to what might have been considered a closed subject.

The man steeped in Fundamentalism his first thirty years discarded narrow conviction to champion broad interpretations of his gospel and social justice in his world. In China he listened to the Chinese and pressed for the Chinese Church to be run for and by Chinese in their own way. In America he was an activist pastor decades before that term was coined. When he died recently at the age of 103, his qualities of steadfastness and forgiveness were stressed by those who attested their lives had been changed by his.

Paul G. Hayes was called many names in his time: Lebzelter's Donkey by smiling neighbors who watched a young boy pushing wheelbarrows; Pop by his college classmates, so much younger than he; Modernist, Heretic or Brother Hayes by his church and mission associates, according to how they felt about his theology; Mr. Big Nose, Teacher Hu and Foreign Devil by the Chinese.

Lebzelter's Donkey is my favorite. During my donkey-riding days in China and the Middle East I came to the conclusion that the gentleness and willingness of these small beasts have often been overlooked because of a more conspicuous trait, usually identified as stubbornness, which can also be interpreted as the intelligence to see more than one possibility in a situation and refusal to go ahead until direction is clear. I am glad these qualities earned my father his nickname at Lebzelter's Bending Works in Lancaster, Pennsylvania, where after his father's death, when he was but ten, he spent six years cleaning spittoons, pushing wheelbarrows, keeping accounts, and learning business fundamentals.

What an immense cultural distance from China he was born into. His heritage was Irish and German, for whom life was serious and hard, even in that "garden spot of America." Family and friends breathed in Christianity with every breath they took, parents and grandparents having fled the "horrors of religious bigotry" in Europe. There were more than thirty-five different sects in Lancaster, some of them enemies in Europe who not only tolerated each other in their new land, but cooperated, and all his life my father moved with ease from one church to another while never giving up his membership in the Methodist Church. At the heart of his life sounded those compelling words to "Go ye into all the world . . ." with the message of compassion and God's love, a message that gained power and meaning through sharing it with others. Missionary names were as familiar to my father when he was a boy as were those of his North Queen and Lemon Street neighbors. Missionary talks were community highlights.

Before he was ten my father heard Henry Appenzeller, Sr., tell of his work in Korea, shortly before he lost his life in an accident there. My father was a small boy, Appenzeller a big man. "I was impressed by his sheer size," my father recalled, "but even more by this wonderful man doing God's work far from his home. I decided when I grew up I would be just like him."

Conservative Christian piety with "no room for new thought," hard physical labor and respect for education marked family life in nineteenth century Lancaster. Both my father's parents, Zachariah and Emma Hayes, were born into farm families, but Zach didn't like farming and chopped cordwood for a time in Nebraska before returning to Lancaster to apprentice as a carriage body maker. Emma, whose mother was killed at a railroad crossing when she was four, was soon placed as a domestic in other farm families by her father, then in a mill when her father moved to Lancaster as a cobbler. Neither Zach nor Emma had more than a country school education, but Zach was a constant reader and read aloud to Emma, creating the climate of ideas so surrounding my father's early years that his greatest boyhood desire was to live in a roomful of books.

Family life revolved around the First Methodist Church, while in public school teachers were permitted to include their Christian witness, and my father counted second only to his mother his fourth grade teacher, Lola Zug, in influencing him toward Christian ministry. In her classroom, where she installed her own pump organ, he learned the great hymns of the church that he belted out in his strong but hardly musical voice every day afterwards. It was in Lola Zug's room that he dropped his pennies into a jug for China Famine Relief. It was in Lola Zug's room that he blew a whistle while hiding behind an open book. Carefully preserved report cards rate him top in everything except conduct, and Miss Zug took care of that. "Whoever blew that whistle will come forward, face the blackboard and remain there until dismissed!" Miss Zug rapped out, adding, "Paul! I expected better than that from you, a Christian boy!" It was in Lola Zug's room he resolved to be better, for he was a Christian boy.

Zach's death in 1900 when my father was ten threw the support of the family on Emma, who took in wash, sewed for neighbors, kept chickens, canned farm produce from relatives, and rented out Zach's workshop and rooms to boarders. But bills accumulated through illness and death compelled her to look for gainful employment for her son, who gave her half his few weekly dollars from selling papers. She taught him to budget the other half, laying aside first the tithe he owed to God. Through friends he found work at Lebzelter's Bending Works, cleaning spittoons and trundling heavy loads to a railway siding until his abilities were recognized and he became a bookkeeper. Eventually he was trusted with the books for three separate ventures under Lebzelter ownership: the bending works itself, the first auto dealership in Lancaster and the Eagle Lumber Company in Virginia, which cut and processed oak, hickory and ash and sold carload lots to the railroads for ties and bridges.

Stories of those early years are rooted in the serious business of helping to support his home and in learning to deal with his sins, to which he often alluded in his Line-A-Day dairy. They seem to have been nothing more than the normal stirrings in an adolescent boy. He missed his father and poured into his diary his sense of that loss and his secret fear that he failed to live up to being the Christian boy he was expected to be. At fourteen he was seized by the urge to respond to the invitation to seek forgiveness of sins that was part of Wednesday night prayer meetings, and this general public acknowledgment of secret troubles opened the way to further healing in a church membership class where he was required to learn many scriptural passages, among them I John 1:9 (*"If we confess our sins, he [God] is faithful and just to forgive us our sins, and to cleanse us from all unrighteousness"*). He examined his sins more closely, confessing in private prayer what he understood them to be, and there entered his heart a lightening of spirit recognized by an elderly leader of his weekly Bible class, who called on him for his word of testimony. Emotionally overcome for the first of few times in his life, grasping a post to get to his feet while tears of joy coursed down his cheeks, he gave his first witness for Christ.

The cumulative power of these experiences became the directing force of his life. It led him one Sunday evening in 1907, when he and his friends usually went looking for fun, into an ice cream parlor with a sign on its entrance reading, "Gospel Mission, All Welcome." The speaker of the evening aimed his powerful message at the newcomer, galvanizing the young man to his feet in witness that Christ had washed him clean of sin.

This was the start of my father's ten-year relationship with the Gospel Mission, in which he became a leader, preached on street corners, took the message of Christ into private homes during weekly cottage meetings, helped organize the mission with a constitution and finally, as its superintendent while a college senior, helped reorganize it as the Water Street Mission, an interdenominational society with ties to all the county churches. It continues to be a community force today.

At many of its meetings people "received the power of the Spirit," shaking and speaking in tongues as my father never felt moved to do. He was more inclined to relate his inner experience of joy and conviction to some practical human need, and started in 1917, with Herman Molin, a service that made it a vital rescue mission reaching annually into hundreds of lives with its spiritual message coupled to practical help.

Herman, a panhandler, knelt at the altar beside a woman of dubious reputation who had been repeatedly saved, as she enjoyed shivering and shaking and coming "under the power," which my father feared might disturb Herman, whom he sensed to be serious. When he asked her to calm down, it was too much for Sarah Kuhns, a woman of little education but deep piety in whose home the mission had begun. She was praying aloud, and in her prayer sidetracked, on hearing my father's whispered request, to ask, "Lord, help him not to touch thine anointed!"

My father took Herman home that night, next day gave him breakfast and went surety for his room and board at a nearby boarding house, then found him employment, an act of trust, Herman said later, that changed his life.

Through his discovery of the mission, my father also discovered the Christian Missionary Alliance, whose young people were workers there. They invited him to their services, which emphasized "Jesus Christ, Savior, Sanctifier, Healer and Glorious Coming King." My father added to his inquisitive mind the idea of the Second Coming, examining all Biblical references, and was deeply convinced.

When he was seventeen he purchased a new Bible and on its flyleaf inscribed, "I am happy in Jesus because I know that God for Christ's sake forgave me my sins. I have consecrated my life to his work and this book shall be used to give the Gospel to those who do not know that Christ died for them."

By the age of nineteen he was a high school dropout supporting his mother and sister, who in turn supported his decisions to be a missionary and to search for appropriate schooling. But other family members were indignant with what they saw as his lack of responsibility. His Aunt Lily wrote from Indiana that she was ashamed he would leave his "little home . . . gotten through hard struggle," and counseled him to use good hard common sense and find his missionary work in caring for his mother and sister. His Aunt Belinda and her husband, a contractor in California, warned him that missionaries and ministers were regarded as dependents, that Chinese were the equal of Westerners if not their superiors in intelligence, that no matter how fine a missionary he might become, the Chinese would not adopt his faith because they could see the unspeakable cruelty with which Christian people treat the helpless. My father has forgotten how he answered, but we know what he did. He continued to support his home until his sister graduated from high school and took over that support.

At a loss to know where to go for missionary training, he one day picked up a small gospel weekly carrying an advertisement for the Union Missionary Training Institute (UMTI) in Brooklyn, which claimed to prepare candidates for the mission field in two years in an atmosphere true to the Bible, interdenominational and coeducational. Believing this to be a direct answer to prayer, he left Lebzelter's on 30 June 1910, turning his back on a business career, and said good-bye to his mother and sister, never expecting to see them again.

There followed an intense year of study, a happy year with like-minded students in a familiar devotional atmosphere, but he became increasingly distressed that returned missionaries trained at UMTI failed to match Appenzeller's presence and authority. His ethics professor agreed, and counseled him to make up his high school work and go to college, then prepare for China. This suggestion was seconded by the Board of Foreign Missions of the Methodist Church in New York, which he hadn't known existed and which he now approached for further guidance.

He walked across the Brooklyn Bridge to 150 Fifth Avenue, where he was bewildered by the huge offices, but was finally led to Dr. George M. Fowles, then both Treasurer and Personnel Secretary, who put his advice in this form: he took a piece of paper and wrote down a two when my father felt sure he could finish high school in two years. Then he put down a four, which stood for college. But then he added a three, which my father did not understand.

"That means seminary," said Dr. Fowles. Nine years of work. "Young man, our Board does not send out missionaries until they have had adequate training."

"But I will be twenty-one this year, the heathen are dying and I am sitting here studying!"

He never forgot nor ceased to be thankful for Dr. Fowles' reply, "You can do all that work and be finished by the time you are thirty, and you will not have sense enough to be a missionary before then."

My father went home to Lancaster to enroll at Franklin & Marshall Academy, a mile walk out Lemon Street from his home, followed by Franklin & Marshall College. The next six years carried him into leadership roles in his classes and in many extracurricular activities, chief among them the Student Volunteer Movement. Some of his classmates accused him of reviving "old fogeyism" at F&M, a criticism "I glory in," he wrote, "for I perceive my fellow students recognize . . . I stand by and contend for the orthodox faith from which so many have departed." He applauded Billy Sunday when the evangelist mounted a chair on top of a table where he took off his coat and waved it in the air shouting, "If your ancestors were monkeys in the tops of tall trees throwing down coconuts, you are no relative of mine!"

While in college my father continued to work with the Gospel Mission and was appointed first pastor of the Ross Street Methodist Church. Entrance of the United States into the First World War changed his preaching. While it was still centered in salvation, he could not escape issues that war raised for the Christian. Convinced his country had entered the war from high motives and able to find Old Testament passages in defense of war, he was perplexed by New Testament conflicts with the Old and came to believe he as a Christian could not enter military service.

Stimulated by the high goals set by President Wilson, he chose the theme, "The Interdependence of Nations" for the Marshall Oration, the college's highest honor at graduation. On the great day he got through the first three paragraphs only to have his mind take off on the last, much to the delight of restive seniors and his own chagrin. But before leaving the campus, he received a letter from his college president commending him for being "one of the best students that has ever gone through this institution," and for his "unusually strong influence for good." Then opening his college annual he read, "And now comes Hayes, our 'grand old man' is he; learned, efficient and of actual worth, gibes are but pointless, and wit misses fire against the shield of his strong probity."

At his side through his F&M years was Mary Zwally. They had met at the Mission, become engaged, and by the end of his senior year had been interviewed and favorably received by the Methodist Board of Foreign Missions, meeting all requirements but seminary. But which seminary?

"How about Drew?" suggested the president of Drew who was on the mission board personnel committee.

"Drew's fine," encouraged his own pastor who was an alumnus.

"Absolutely not," roared Dr. L.W. Munhall, a lay evangelist. "Read my book, *Methodists Adrift. Breakers Ahead!* All our seminaries have deviated from Methodist theology. Drew once was good but has fallen from Grace. Iliff is terrible, but Boston! Boston is worst of all!"

"Paul, you go to Boston and find out for yourself!" the answer came to him, he believed as the voice of God. He applied, was accepted, and gained approval for his marriage before enrolling.

Their first year at Boston University School of Theology was a happy one for my father and Mary, but a widespread epidemic of Spanish influenza was part of the high cost of the war, and my father's duties in Malden, where he was a student pastor, increased with the multiplication of patients until he, then Mary, succumbed. He recovered, to pray for a miracle of healing for Mary, who was pregnant and not given much chance by their doctor. But she died. Stunned, my father returned to Lancaster to bury her and was immediately caught up in caring for his sister Rhoda, also sick with flu, and for his mother, long suffering from Bright's disease, who collapsed while doing the laundry. They recovered and he busied himself with visitors and house repairs while gradually coming to understand that his experience identified him with the common lot of mankind, which in later years helped him to lay up his heart with others in their sorrows.

Gradually he came to realize that the faith which he preached and to which he testified was true. God was with him. He returned to dismantle the small rooms he and Mary had made their home, to pick up his studies, hardly able to take in the celebration of the Armistice. It was a hard second year. The third began well, only to precipitate him once more into the shock of loss. Emma died.

Father. Wife. Mother. A thinking person threatened by feeling that washed over him unchecked in the pileup of loss, this serious young man in a three-piece suit, Phi Beta Kappa key dangling from his watch chain, was poised on the brink of further change. He was ready for an idea great enough to succor him from sorrow. His professors provided it.

Not once doubting his faith he welcomed their challenge to accept the spirit of unfettered inquiry and subjected his convictions to the most searching questions, discarding every fanciful interpretation that he now felt did violence to the spirit of Jesus.

Absorbed by the excitement generated through Dr. Albert Knudson, who introduced him to modern Biblical research and literary criticism, tools his mind was ready to accept and use, he wrote his thesis on a comparison of Chronicles with Samuel and Kings. These months of research yielded the insight that the Word of God in the Scriptures, every word of it, had come through the minds and preconceptions of men. For a man nearly thirty in 1919, steeped in Fundamentalism, this was a breakthrough into glorious understanding. But when it came to making a choice between the missionary call from his youth and the more recent discovery that scholarly research and teaching held a deep appeal for him, he did not hesitate to turn down a fellowship in Germany which would have led to a theological teaching career.

He delayed his departure for China one more year after seminary, feeling the need for further grounding in Biblical scholarship and to be with his sister her first year at Boston University. He lived at the seminary with other single men, developing friendships that lasted his lifetime, broadening his experiences of the historical and cultural treasures of Boston, preaching at nearby churches on weekends and working in a barrel factory in Fremont, New Hampshire to pay his way.

He had been in touch at intervals with the Methodist Board of Foreign Missions, but his appointment had been left unsettled by his electing this further year of study. In April 1921 a letter from a Board secretary informed him that his type of mind was "dangerous to send to the mission field," a comment that baffled him, and nothing was said about his appointment. Shaken, he withdrew his application, only to receive a letter in June directing him to attend a conference for new missionaries and to sail for China in August from San Francisco.

On 14 July he set out on the three-week journey he had planned between Lancaster and San Francisco, seeing by rail the immensity and diversity of his country that he had expected to see with Mary. He toured most of America's greatest scenic attractions and historical sites, visited with friends and relatives, learned all he could about the homes, schools, churches, agriculture, business and industry of his country. Determined not to miss a thing, on an ostrich farm in California he took the reins to a light buggy and drove a bird around a race track. On an alligator farm, challenged by the guard, he sat on the back of one of the big reptiles and lifted its jaw while cameras snapped. Little did he know that in Chicago, also en route to China, Helen Wolf was taking a ride in an airplane, determined not to be "out of it" when she returned to America, convinced that by her furlough everyone would be flying around in planes.

August 10 was sailing day for the *Korea Maru*, a slow boat carrying freight for Honolulu, Yokohama, Kobe and Nagasaki as well as a lively collection of missionaries. As departure time approached the band played, visitors left the ship, paper streamers stretched from deck to pier neared the breaking point as the gap widened between them, when suddenly a woman on the pier to whom my father had been introduced on deck cupped her hands and shouted, "Mr. Hayes! There's a girl on board going to Nanking Language School too!" He stepped back from the rail as she repeated her shout to Helen Wolf, who also stepped back to acknowledge the introduction.

My father was intrigued by the vivacious, wavy-haired, blue-eyed young woman who passed around chocolates, threw herself into games of shuffleboard and ping-pong, and joined a group of lighthearted young missionaries at their dining table when she found the table to which she had been assigned too stuffy. He acknowledged to himself that part of the reason he had stayed at Boston University a further year was in the hope of finding a wife to go to China with him, but had not found a new love. The lady we were to know as Sally had followed him to Boston after Mary's death and tried to attract him in various ways. When all else failed, she asked his help to plan her class schedule. When it was worked out to her satisfaction and he rose to go, she exclaimed, "Paul! You don't understand!" Taken aback as she insisted God had told her to go to China as his wife, he stuttered that God hadn't said a word to him about it, and fled. Now he wondered whether God were speaking that word. For her part, Helen Wolf was intrigued by the solemn young preacher she questioned about the virgin birth and evolution, whose answers made more sense than others she had heard.

Her adroit theological questions soon had them talking about other matters, and my father learned that when he was starting school she had been born the seventh of fourteen children to Samuel and Ida Bryan Wolf in Bethlehem, Pennsylvania. Samuel, a studious and artistic young man, was for a time a carpenter and teacher, later accountant for the Lehigh Valley Railroad. He was brought up in the prominent Fackenthal family of lawyers and educators, and had married their Irish maid.

My parents each inherited the neat, hard-working, practical and deeply religious values of their German forbears; my father the dourness of his German mother, Mother the gaiety of her Irish mother. Growing up in a large family, Mother's naturally fun-loving nature flourished, and as she moved out into her community it was channeled into its only social outlet, the Reformed Church in the United States, where for many years her father was Sunday School superintendent. He was responsible for bringing in missionary speakers and for the "double envelope" offerings in which Mother placed five cents each week for local expenses and two cents for missions. When Mr. Stanley spoke in Easton about the work of Livingston in Africa, Sam Wolf chose Helen from among his children to accompany him to the lecture.

But it was the young returned missionaries full of strange and exciting tales of faraway lands, usually China, who attracted her most. When she was fifteen she sold peanuts to raise the money she needed to attend a summer institute where a group of these young missionaries sat around one evening telling stories and teasing one another. She determined to be one of these "real people."

When she announced she was going to China, "Tell your mother," said the father who never quite knew what to do with his huge flock of children and turned prickly questions over to Ida.

"Well, I guess not! You'll finish school first!" said her mother. My mother finished high school and taught in a one-room schoolhouse where many of her students were bigger and older than she was. One evening Ida came to her as she was brushing out her long hair and, watching her daughter's eyes light up in the mirror, said slowly, "At church this morning I heard Helen Ammerman speak about her work with Bible women in Yochow. She is staying here to get married and is trying to find someone to take her place. You may go to China now, if you want."

Mother spun around to hug her mother, dashed off a letter to her church mission board, then followed their advice to finish out her school year before going to the Kennedy School of Missions in Hartford. Backing her when she sailed for China was a group of her friends at St. Andrew Reformed Church in Allentown, Pennsylvania, who had organized themselves into the Helen Mae Wolf Missionary Society.

Mother listened to the story of my father's boyhood, education and marriage with a growing realization of how much fun he had missed, and determined to make it up to him. My father searched his heart, too. On 5 September 1921, when the *Korea Maru* crossed mud flats through a sea yellow with Yangtze River water to anchor at Woosung, they stood together at the rail for their first sight of Shanghai.

With the Boston Brown Bag beside her, Mother guards the luggage on a Yangtze steamer with her trusty umbrella, her shield against sun and rain, her weapon against would-be thieves.

Paul G. Hayes

Missionaries' light-hearted sides found many outlets enroute to China. Most got into the dunking and pillow fight rituals in the ship's canvas pool when crossing the International Date Line. My father had his picture taken on a dare seated on a huge alligator, and here he drove an ostrich around a California race track.

My parents in 1920 look rather solemn as they anticipate their serious mission ahead. But I remember a lot of laughter and good-humored kidding throughout my childhood.

Mother with resting camel train by Peking wall.

Paul G. Hayes

Sailing Tung Ting Lake near Yochow, Mother's original destination which my parents visited on their honeymoon. The junk was more comfortable than the railway boxcar they rode from steamer to city.

Paul G. Hayes

Formidable Questions

s my parents went together to get their trunks through Shanghai customs and were surrounded for the first time by the ragged, shouting, good-natured but dying coolies who were to haunt their years in China, they knew the characters for coolie mean "bitter strength," but were unprepared to see in thin wasted bodies the actual meaning of these words. As my father handed over the few coppers they demanded, he was struck by how impossible it might be to preach Christ's gospel of goodwill to the undernourished and overburdened.

They arrived in China in the tenth year of the new Republic, when footbinding was still in fashion and back in the countryside many had not yet heard that queues, symbolizing subservience to the Manchus, had been ordered cut off in 1911. Familiar spirits were summoned to tell fortunes or to work spells for healing the sick, the Kitchen God graced most households and ancestors' graves were swept regularly. They arrived when blue eyes were still thought by some to rivet one with evil, when foreign doctors were still sometimes suspected of taking Chinese children's eyes to combine with mercury to make silver.

In the late nineteenth century China had suffered humiliating defeats by the Russians in Manchuria, the French in Indo-China, the Japanese in Korea and Formosa, while Great Britain, France, Germany and the United States each had a toehold on her seaports. Especially humiliated

51

by defeat from Japan, long considered a barbarian country dependent on China for her culture, Chinese noted that Japan's victory came largely through use of techniques borrowed from the West, and looked to the same source for rejuvenation, sending their young men to Japan, Germany, Russia, England and the United States for training.

By the time my parents were on the scene, Chinese nationalism in a modern sense had been born. But 1921 was still a time of confusion, the country grandly disunited with only a fragile facade of officials trying to meet recurring disasters. The revolution that ended the Ch'ing dynasty had set up a Republic with Dr. Sun Yat-sen as president, but it was not strong enough to control provincial governors who became warlords fighting each other to extend their powers. Landlords continued to oppress people, and poverty was so extensive that millions were said to be starving while a small elite looked on with apparent indifference.

My father knew this general picture from his reading, but did not know that simultaneously there was a second dimension to the revolution. While he and Mother had been packing for their journey, on 1 July 1921 the first Congress of the Chinese Communist Party was organized by twelve people in Shanghai. No one could have predicted that within twenty-eight years the entire country would celebrate the end of the revolution and would credit it to Communists.

My parents had ten days in Shanghai to get acquainted with mission banking procedures, get two palmbeach suits tailored for my father and to explore the city. They knew Shanghai was a great commercial port, one of five opened to foreign trade after the Opium Wars (1839-1842) when the original village on the Yangtze flats was surrounded by the great Western city built by the French, Russians, Americans and British, but chiefly by the British. They expected the Western appearance of the business center, found it true that foreigners had taken advantage of their privileges to develop trade agreements in their own interests, that gambling and prostitution were openly encouraged. They had heard that among the many rules posted at the entrance to a Shanghai park was, "Chinese and dogs not allowed." But when they checked it out the sign read in one instance, "Chinese not allowed unless accompanied by a foreigner." Elsewhere dogs were banned.

My father was fascinated by the cosmopolitan city, offended by the foreign control which he likened to Chinese, Japanese or Russian business interests running New York or Chicago. When he saw a Sikh traffic cop whack a coolie on the head with his club he warned in his journal that "some day China will rise up and shake that octopus off, will crush to death that blood sucking leech — unless we foreigners see the situation and correct it before it is too late."

Revolutions of any kind require a great deal of tedious work, and the spiritual revolution in which my parents were enlisted required a full year of language study. At the Nanking Language School, a joint effort of a number of Protestant missions which was in its tenth year, they plunged into the lessons that, to echo William Milne a hundred years earlier, demanded "a head of oak, eyes of an eagle, lungs of brass, fingers of sprung steel, patience of Job and the years of Methuselah."

Taught by the direct method without English, within a few weeks they could give directions to rickshaw pullers and shop on their own. My father, not blessed with a good ear, joined the "dumbbell class" for additional practice, then braved the streets to try his luck. Noting one day an easing of the throngs that slowed his impatient step when someone ahead of him shouted, *"Lu-tzu lai le! Lu-tzu lai le!"* he repeated the shout. Gratified that the traffic parted before him, he was suddenly suspicious when those who stepped aside and glanced back at him broke into laughter. Later he asked an older missionary what it was he had said, and learned he hadn't noticed the small cavalcade the shout had announced: "The donkeys are coming!"

It was the kind of mistake made by all newcomers, and hardly compared, in his mind, to his gaffe when he first preached in Chinese and for the polite salutation, "I, your younger brother," was told he had announced himself, "I, the Lord God."

Supplementing classes was a wealth of cultural experiences giving the newcomers some appreciation of China's vast history, culture and religions. My parents realized how ignorant they were of China's ancient philosophies and customs, and set out to learn all they could.

Theirs was the third of three generations of Protestant missionaries in China. Pearl Buck understood the first and second generation "missionary warriors," quarrelsome men like her father, Andrew Sydenstricker, who "chose the greatest god he knew, and set forth into the universe to make men acknowledge his god to be the one true God, before whom all must bow." She saw this as a "magnificent imperialism of the spirit, incredible and not to be understood except by those who have been reared up in it, and have grown beyond it."

Those first and second generation Protestant missionaries believed without doubt in the superiority of Christianity, that Buddhism and Tao-ism were made up of misguided superstitions, that while Confucianism might enable men to live within set patterns of human relationships, it ignored sin. And in truth, the manifestations of ancient Chinese philoso-phies they most often met were crude superstitions, for they were largely cut off from intelligent discourse with gentry and officials schooled in Chinese classics who were equally persuaded of their own superior un-derstandings, contemptuous of the humble and ignorant people convert-ing to Christianity. The missionaries did not understand the role in Chinese society played by either gentry or officials, nor did they rise often enough above the human tendency to compare the best in their own religion with the worst in others. The Chinese did not understand that Christianity throve on persecution, and little of the Buddhist tradi-tion of disinterested service survived into the twentieth century, so that what common ground there might have been, to lesson suspicions of missionary motives, was gone.

Missionaries arrived with their message of salvation from sin among a people steeped for centuries in the attitude behind the opening lines of the *San-tzu-ching:* "The nature of man at the beginning is good." They found plenty of sin in the limited sense of Western morality, plenty of sin in the broad sense of profit from exploitation of human misery and need. "Millions of Chinese," mourned my father as he looked around him, "discarded like so many old shoes when they are exhausted, dying with-out having eaten a decent meal, much less having known their own worth or experienced an inner sense of redemption."

The early missionaries were slow to realize that most Chinese identi-fied them with the traders in opium and the prostitution that proliferated wherever foreign soldiers or businesses settled. Appalled by Westerners, the Chinese tried to drive them away by frustrating or frightening them, their opposition giving way reluctantly as China suffered military defeats at the hands of the West.

The second generation of missionaries found the Chinese clergy made up largely of men who had been coolies, gatemen or servants in mission homes, who delighted in their new importance as preachers.

Scholars of the second generation, like Andrew Sydenstricker, were shocked that Chinese representatives of their faith should be looked down upon by educated Chinese, and gathered young intellectuals about them to discuss history and philosophy. For trusting to the power of men's brains rather than to the power of God, they were condemned by their elders as heretics, liberals and modernists.

Yet in turn they denounced as heretics, liberals and modernists those of my parents' generation who came to believe that the spirit of loving kindness mattered more than creeds, that a Chinese Church freed from Western influences was more important than dogmas or denominations, more important than the continued presence of missionaries. My parents' generation was one that studied, respected and learned to appreciate Chinese values and institutions. Indeed, what distinguished this generation was awareness among many that Christianity was a foreign implant about to be rejected unless it could be transformed into Chinese. But it was a generation that did not speak with one voice, and the conflict between liberal and conservative was sometimes a bitter one.

There were one hundred eleven members of the 1921-1922 Language School class, representing a dozen churches in America, Canada, England and Germany. Most were educators, others doctors, nurses, administrators, secretaries, librarians, musicians, YMCA, YWCA and social workers, specialists in agriculture, animal husbandry or physical education. Only seventeen were evangelists. My father was quickly aware that a majority of his classmates were strong in the Fundamentalism of his youth, and listened silently to those who spoke of modern theology as work of the devil, of the community church idea as Satanic alchemy.

While in Language School he lived in the home of Harry F. Rowe, Acting President of the University of Nanking and Dean of its Seminary in 1921, one of the "big four" who had shaped development of this successful union of several missions in higher education for more than a quarter century. All four men (who included Wilbur Fisk Wilson, Vice President and Dean of the College of Liberal Arts as well as of the Language School in 1921; Arthur J. Bowen, first President of the University, credited with much of the initiative that established it; and Edward James, for more than twenty years Evangelist in Central China who spent another twenty teaching at the Seminary), were good sources of information about Nanking, mission practices and history and current Chinese affairs, information my father shared with Mother as they explored Nanking streets and strolled her great wall.

While my father learned history and gathered facts, Mother looked about her and was startled to realize she had been plunged into scenes straight out of the Bible: women drawing water from a well, the city wall, the watch towers, men driving herds of pigs and goats, others riding donkeys, priests in their long robes, lepers and beggars and the blind begging in the streets and temple courtyards. She tried to talk to people and felt rebuffed by the solid wall of courtesy. On Christmas Eve, stunned to see no signs of festivity, she suddenly realized how much of the world was unaware of the story she had come to tell.

On 13 June 1922, surrounded by their now beloved host families and classmates, my parents were married in Sage Chapel at the University of Nanking. "Bought and paid for, like a Chinese bride," quipped Mother, when the Methodist Board of Foreign Missions reimbursed her Reformed Church Board for her travel, salary and training.

After visiting Yochow, where Mother had originally been assigned, and a summer spent on Lushan (the beautiful central China mountain where one could escape the deadly heat of the Yangtze valley) continuing their language study, they took a river steamer to Wuhu. There my father was quickly comfortable with his Chinese neighbors who, like those in Lancaster, were farmers and shopkeepers. But their poverty, their helplessness at the hands of ruthless authorities, were of a magnitude beyond his experience.

He soon discovered how little his fellow missionaries knew of the life of the city, immersed as they were in demanding, often overwhelming, jobs, and without the special ability needed to read the *Wan-chiang*, the daily paper. He bought the paper and extracted its major news with the help of his secretary/teacher and learned that a General Wang, who was probably appointed by the Anhwei military governor, occupied the *yamen*, the local seat of government, and had jurisdiction over the southern half of the province. That General Wang had the power of life and death was soon brought home to him. One day en route to the city church on *Erh ma-lu*, Second Street, he passed crowds of people gathered along a railway cut where no rails had yet been laid, which was to serve as execution grounds for three criminals, bound and gagged and under guard. On his return he saw the bloody marks in the dirt and bought a paper to find out why they had been killed.

He learned they had been accused as brigands, that before execution one had had his eyes put out and his private parts cut off which he had been forced to eat in public. Shocked he looked up the criminal code with the help of his secretary and found the executions had clearly been in violation of it. Other executions followed, the mother of one luckless youth admitting her son was a beggar but had been accused of theft and rape. There was no public outcry against such acts where the military had a stranglehold and the courts were largely powerless.

A complete greenhorn in China, my father's first appointment was as evangelist and district superintendent of the Methodist Episcopal Central China Mission, work of which he was entirely ignorant. An inappropriate appointment, he thought, but since the current district superintendent was long overdue for a furlough and there was no one else to take his place, my father set out to discover what his duties were. They were not spelled out, but he had observed superintendents at work in America and instructions on the office in the *Discipline* specified how he should maintain the spiritual vitality and extent of the Christian community within his care and encourage pastors and people to spread the gospel message to the many thousands who had not yet heard it. With his nose for statistics, he soon learned that although mission work in Wuhu was now forty years old, only about 600 people had been drawn from its population of some 200,000 by all the missions put together.

There were fifteen churches and outposts in his district, which included Wuhu and much of southern Anhwei, but were so scattered as to require four or five trips spaced across several months to reach them all. He was eager to do so and soon learned that most of the churches had less than a hundred members each. The total number of members of all fifteen varied from year to year, but did not pass 900 during his administration, about the membership, he realized, of his home church in Lancaster.

The three Ichishan doctors accompanied him on trips that did not reach all of his churches but gave him valuable experience in learning how to travel in China, how to acquire food and lodgings. Frank Gaunt introduced him to the Ichishan church, then took him to Silian-shan, T'ai ping-fu and Tsai shi-chi, where Dr. Gaunt demonstrated the missionary trick, in the absence of beds, of taking a door off its hinges, placing it across two *pan teng*, carpenter's horses used as chapel seats, and spreading his beddingroll on top. Robert Brown took him by rickshaw to Second Street Church where he met Pastor Li Kwoh-ling with whom he felt an immediate rapport. By launch, my father accompanied Robert Brown upriver to Tikan, where the doctor gave a stereopticon slide health lecture, and on to Hwanghu on foot so that the doctor could hunt deer and pheasant along the way. They stopped at a farmhouse to purchase rice and vegetables for lunch and were taken to be Japanese workers from a nearby mine.

Walter Libby took him on a five day trip to Chaohsien, north of the Yangtze, where he had been called to tend a sick missionary child, then on to Yuintsao. During the rainy season, this trip started with a sampan ride across the Yangtze, a moonlight houseboat ride up a tributary to a village, then seventy *li*, about twenty-three miles, overland on foot along deeply muddied roads, crossing two swollen streams in round wooden tubs paddled by farmers' wives, and two others by sampan.

He took readily to the steam launches, sailboats and sampans he so often had to use, but balked at riding in man-powered wheelbarrows or rickshaws, and walked a great deal. Pastor Li Kwoh-ling often walked with him. A man of about forty with five children, Pastor Li came from a Yuintsao family, his parents landowners and in comfortable circumstances when they had converted to Christianity some thirty years earlier. They joined from belief, not material need; indeed they provided, as Pastor Li was often to do, funds to support church programs. Pastor Li had a reputation for integrity among older missionaries who had known him as a student at the University of Nanking and Seminary, and it was easy to see he was beloved by his congregation.

My father found this older man intellectually stimulating and spiritually helpful as a preacher, and listened carefully to accounts of his years supervising Chinese coolies in France during the First World War, of his fifteen years as a village pastor. He took to Li the question that intensified with his experience: Why don't the Chinese churches grow?

Pastor Li explained that many Chinese joined the churches because they saw the missionaries as a source of rice or clothing, of education or protection against ill-treatment by local officials, of help in obtaining better jobs; sometimes as a gesture of gratitude for favors done.

"Don't they join because they want to be saved from their sins?" my father persisted. "What is there about the church that makes people think it can satisfy only worldly desires?"

He learned that the Western church idea of self support merely irritated the Chinese who resented pressures for financial support. They did not understand why they were being pressed, expecting that the Church would require their obedience but not their leadership.

It was obvious that some church members gambled, drank and smoked opium. Presently my father began to hear charges of sexual misconduct, that one pastor lent out parts of his salary at ruinous rates to poor farmers and did not hesitate to take all or part of the fields of those in default. He took his misgivings to a Chinese evangelist leading campaigns in his district, who did not hesitate to confirm the formidable list, and added that many had had no personal experience of Christ and did not attend church regularly, blamed others for their shortcomings and expected the church to aid them in lawsuits.

My father could readily pick out those pastors whose lives had been transformed through their Christian experience. There weren't many. He was especially fond of Pastor Koh Wen-chuin, whose story began when he was a child, the son of a peddler of geese and chickens, rice and vegetables, who traveled the countryside then relaxed with his opium pipe. Two older brothers had died as children, and Koh was close to his mother, a devout Buddhist, whom he accompanied to the temple. But his mother died, and when his father was on the road the boy was alone and miserable. One day he was attracted by lights and music to the hall of the foreign devils he had been told not to enter, but his burdened heart drove him inside where he found only a kindly Chinese gentleman who spoke convincingly of a divine being who said over and again, "Come unto me and I will give you rest."

"Does that mean me?" he asked after the others had left, and assured it did he became an inquirer. Within two years he was baptized, his potential for Christian service was recognized, and he was enabled to go to Nanking, the city of his dreams, where for six years he studied in a Bible school and worked as a nurse's aid before going on to further studies and a license to preach.

When Koh and his wife and children first arrived at the North Anhwei village of Muhsi, he was recognized as a leader with a message of hope. He had taken with him an organ, and when he began to sing and pray and preach, the place was jammed with people. With castor oil, carbolic acid and clean bandages he was soon performing what seemed to be miracles of healing. The number of inquirers increased and in a surprisingly short time enough money was collected to buy land with the hope of building a church. Then enthusiasm tapered off and nothing was done.

Such stories were a part of every missionary's experience, and they found it not unusual for Bible stories, tracts and pictures illustrating Christian values to be completely misinterpreted. Typical is the tale of two Chinese women looking at a picture of an apostle, staff in hand, about to enter a door opened to him by a woman with a child clinging to her skirts. The apostle with hand upraised in blessing says, "Peace be to this house." Peering at the picture and unable to read, one woman asks the other what it means, and the other explains, "Don't you see, in the West it is the same as in China. The master has been from home and the first thing he does on his return is to beat his poor wife."

My father reported on his first round of his district that he paid salaries, settled differences, investigated charges. He found it unnecessary to include the "false charge against Pastor Peng, the unfortunate and irreconcilable differences between Pastor Djen and Mr. Ho, or the three times Mr. Sen falsely accused Mr. Chu." Nor did he report the withdrawal of the preacher at Yuintsao when he took a concubine, hoping for a son, nor his sickening suspicion that Pastor Djen had set fire to his own church and parsonage in order to collect the insurance, a charge later substantiated. Ending typically on an upbeat note, he reported to the Annual Conference, "Closer observation showed me the heart of the church, with its living faith, its high morality, and its spirit of Jesus."

As he tried to learn why this array of troubles afflicted his churches, my father read of a survey in the *International Review of Missions* which concluded that many missionaries imparted ideas without making any effort to help Chinese experience a real sense of God as a power to be reckoned with in the practical affairs of life. Daniel J. Fleming, head of Union Theological Seminary Department of Missions, believed that many missionaries went about their work with attitudes that courted failure: they believed in conquest for Christ and ignored what other religions had to say; they believed that ideas springing from their own cultures were true, all others false. My father listened carefully when the few Chinese Christian leaders began to speak out critically against missionary complacency and against the Chinese church for accepting foreign money and foreign thought.

My father believed it was up to him to understand, challenge, change where possible the ways in which his faith was being presented to a people he found to be intelligent and willing to listen. In a characteristic gesture, in which he connected large problems to his own attitudes and actions, he first stripped his own theology down to the single most powerful belief of Christianity in the loving kindness of God, and that man with all his faults is able to conquer them by patterning his life on that of the Christ who came to show him how he could be like God.

There was no necessity for an emotional conversion, he believed, nor to believe that Jesus spoke with the authority of the Son of God, to follow his teachings and create a world that restrained greed, lust, selfishness and fear and strengthened courage, love, self-control, kindness, pity and self-sacrifice.

My father's church was largely progressive, but he found himself most often among Fundamentalists. Soon after his arrival in China he had been taken in hand by older missionaries and had the "way of God expounded more perfectly" to him. He couldn't escape the issue by sitting quietly in a corner reading, as he did on the *Chang-an* making the down river run from Kiukiang in 1923, when an older missionary reached over for his book, *New Churches for Old,* by John Haynes Holmes, who was pastor of the Community Church in New York, founder of the NAACP and Civil Liberties Union. She laid down her knitting and adjusted her spectacles. "By what imaginable reversion of attention," asked Dr. Holmes, "can persons who have learned the lessons of Newton and Darwin, and are now sitting at the feet of Bergson and Einstein, be persuaded to hold interest in affirmations of the Trinity, the Atonement, the Resurrection, Salvation, and the rest — much less to express their spiritual ideals in terms of these conceptions?" Throwing down the book with a bang and picking up her knitting, she declared, "I daren't read that kind of book — it would make me mad!" and followed this up with a lecture.

What were the "fundamentals" creating conflict? Belief in the absence of error from the books of Old and New Testaments. Belief in the necessity of expiation (the extinguishing of guilt through suffering) in order to be forgiven one's sins. Belief that the dependence of future life for man lies in reunion with the body vacated at death, with the return of Jesus in the flesh, no longer as Savior but as Judge.

At the World Fundamentalist Convention held in 1923 in Fort Worth, Texas, it was agreed to withdraw support from schools teaching any form of evolution, to delete such theories from all textbooks and compel all teachers to reaffirm annually their belief in the account of creation in Genesis, in the historical fact of Biblical miracles, the virgin birth, resurrection, the imminent second coming of Christ, the reality of a personal devil and literal hell. It was agreed to pressure state schools to conform to these beliefs, to reject Sunday School lessons diverging from them, to require the resignation of all pastors, evangelists and Sunday School teachers who differed. It required the organization of local fundamental societies in each church for propaganda and the organization of separate schools should their pressure to bring public schools into line with their thinking fail.

There was nothing, my father thought, more calculated to disrupt the practical unity of Christianity, more likely to shipwreck the whole mission enterprise.

He looked for something of value in every sermon he heard, although most preaching, both Chinese and foreign, was Fundamentalist. He drew the line when Fundamentalism became coupled with a vindictive spirit, and he became impatient with inaccurate scholarship. He assured his Fundamentalist friends that they and he based their beliefs on the same Book, the same Lord, and tried to reduce antagonisms by focusing his own sermons on what all Christians could accept.

In prayer he scrutinized his own thoughts and actions, gave greater priority to his devotions that under the stress of work had diminished. He understood the seriousness of the Chinese complaint that missionaries gave too little heed to understanding the cultural history and philosophy of those among whom they worked, and redoubled his own studies. Knowing there were other missionaries who thought as he did, he called on them to reexamine with him the whole Christian mission movement, not anticipating that during his second term the laymen who paid for missions would actually carry out such a study and that he would have a part in it.

There had been no agitation on the part of the Chinese, that he could discover, during the four decades during which the Chinese churches were becoming established, to participate in decisions about budgets or appointments, although some of the missionaries had tried to promote Chinese leadership. But in 1923 and 1924 a number of basic moves were made recognizing that some Chinese were beginning to speak to this question. The Annual Conference was placed on the same level of authority as conferences in the United States, and the powerful Finance Committee was reorganized to include equal numbers of Chinese and foreigners. My father stepped aside so that a Chinese could be appointed district superintendent in his place. Then he wrote to all the missionaries of his Central China Conference urging them to transfer titles of buildings for worship to their local churches, to redouble their efforts to find Chinese willing to take responsibility, and urged that foreign subsidies be reduced.

But budget decreases made in New York as a result of worsening economic life in America were already doing this before Chinese churches were ready to make up the difference. In 1924, following a summer of civil war in the north where two great warlords, Chang Tso-lin and Wu P'ei-fu, jockeyed for control of the northern capital, and sporadic student strikes in other great cities, the New York Board had to reduce apportionments for Chinese pastors' salaries by fifteen percent. Realizing the hardships this decision would bring about, the missionaries voted to have the Chinese salaries made up from their own.

Every time my father glanced out his study windows and saw the warships on the Yangtze, the issues raised for Christian missionaries by foreign powers dominating Chinese commerce were sharpened for him. US ships were on patrol and not based in Wuhu as were the British and Japanese, and despite his reservations over what they represented, he was always excited when the Stars and Stripes hove to for a visit. He enjoyed talking with Americans other than missionaries, and one evening had two sailors from the USS *Villalobos* to dinner, one of them, "from the north, the other south; one Methodist, the other Roman Catholic; both showing their European ancestry in their accent, yet both of them — American." He liked this variety.

But the name of their ship gave him pause. The *Villalobos* was one of three in Chinese waters which were part of American spoil from the

Spanish-American War. My father remembered the day in 1898 when the battleship USS *Maine* was blown up in Havana harbor, and how its destruction fired the American people (who believed in their "Manifest Destiny") into preparation for war, ostensibly to liberate Cuba from Spanish domination but in retrospect including a large dose of injured national pride and desire for revenge.

He was appointed to work in the Yangtze Valley, under the protection of foreign guns, but felt he had no moral right to such protection: "I firmly believe that in the gospel of Jesus I have the thing which China needs, but it will do no good to force it down their throats. If my gospel cannot conquer by its own truth there is something wrong with my gospel."

Most of his sermons were based on the transforming power of Jesus, but the Yangtze warships made him think more carefully about the Christian's attitude toward war. He made a survey of all his sermons in support of the First World War, and was chagrined to find he had labeled war in the abstract as wrong, this particular one as right; that he had found all of the American wars, except the Mexican, justified on the basis of Israel's conquest of Canaan; that he had set Jesus up as a champion of war on flimsy interpretations of texts taken out of context.

He based a new sermon on the great passage in Isaiah 2 and Micah 4, updating the images, of swords beaten into plowshares and spears into pruning hooks, into the changing of dreadnoughts into locomotives and submarines into structural steel. His next sermon unfolded around Jesus' challenge to his disciples to be peacemakers, not just lovers of peace. He called for support of America's entrance into the League of Nations, insisted Christians must face up to the immorality and inconsistency with Christian ideals involved in the support of war.

An ordained missionary and four business people walked out of the Wuhu church during this sermon. He felt sympathetic, for only eighteen months previously when the Quaker, Henry Hodgkin, had been announced as a speaker, his own reaction had been, "I don't want to hear that pacifist." But he had gone to hear Dr. Hodgkin, and his thinking changed. He soon discovered that the outstanding religious leaders of the Western world were all coming out against war as evil, but his stand alienated more of his own colleagues.

Summers on Lushan, the Kiangsi mountain where foreigners from Central China provinces escaped the worst of summer heat, gave my father the opportunity to exchange ideas with Southern Baptists from Louisiana, Southern Presbyterians from Virginia, Methodists from Kansas, Disciples from California, Episcopalians from Boston, Lutherans from Minnesota, London Mission men from Cambridge, Plymouth Brethren from New Zealand.

The missionaries on Lushan had organized themselves into a community with a council to maintain a variety of services centering in a Union Church and an annual Missionary Conference, to which outstanding leaders from Europe and the United States were invited. They had built the church, an auditorium, store, a hospital, an American high school, and a swimming pool, and had a regular transport of coolies up and down the mountain to Lien hua-tung Rest House for supplies.

My father was immediately drawn into administration of the Methodist property. Vested in the Board of Missions as were all mission properties, every dollar for Methodist Valley in Kuling, the name of the small settlement on the mountain, had been contributed by individual missionaries or was the result of careful management. He spent nearly every summer with workmen on house repairs, maintenance of the swimming pool, roads and drains, tennis courts and sanitary facilities; was responsible for financial arrangements, rents, debentures, taxes, insurance. He researched and published a handbook about the Sanitarium, supervised remodeling of two houses into an auditorium, named Beebe Hall, with a lower floor to house Chinese teachers.

He usually took his own Chinese teacher/secretary along to Lushan so as to keep abreast of district business and continue language study. When it rained he read, wrote articles that began to find publication, planned sermons and Bible study courses he was asked to lead.

Of greatest value on Lushan he counted the stimulating give and take during hikes and retreats with men of his own generation wrestling with the same problems that gripped him. And it was on Lushan that some of these exchanges coalesced into an unusually concerted effort to redress wrongs done China at the hands of the West.

In the early 1920s the battle for control of the young Republic was in full swing between the conservative forces of the north under divided leadership, and Western-oriented forces of the south, first under Sun Yatsen followed by Chiang Kai-shek. While the missionaries tried to follow the developments in Chinese affairs that were turning much of their work into chaos, armies of young peasant boys clashed and bled.

There was a slightly comic quality to armies that called off battles when it rained, although that was sensible, given the torrents that turned the countryside into deep mud. There was an appealing flavor to generals given to reading the classics while being carried from battle to battle in sedan chairs. I remember the story of one warlord who promised to win a certain battle or return in his coffin. He was cheered on his return, in defeat, waving and grinning, seated in his coffin borne on the shoulders of his men. But it was a time of tragedy and disaster, not only for the young men dying in battle. The armies lived off the land they fought over, their presence often spelling the difference between life and death for villagers who lived too close to the bone.

The two revolutionary forces, Nationalist and Communist, were slowly gathering for confrontation, while an anti-Christian movement became the focus of xenophobia. By 1925 mission work had been seriously interrupted by agitations and demonstrations, and by peasant sufferings as the villagers caught between rival military forces required first missionary attention. Crop failures and a cholera epidemic brought more disruption. Older missionaries who remembered the Rice Riots of 1910 said the feeling in 1925 was even worse and some packed for evacuation.

On 30 May 1925 the "Shanghai Incident," as the foreign press called it, or the "Shanghai Massacre" as the aroused Chinese called it, shocked the mission community.

What had happened at Shanghai? Unarmed students demonstrated against the killing of a striking laborer, and were fired upon by Settlement police who killed thirteen students. The police were under the protection of extraterritoriality and could not be punished. During the weeks that followed, the country was in an uproar of charges and countercharges, gigantic student parades in every university city, strikes and boycotts of foreign goods, chiefly British. Steamers were held in ports, violence broke out in Hankow, Canton and Kiukiang, with destruction of some foreign property and loss of some foreign lives.

A second incident occurred 23 June when a French gunboat near the British Concession in Canton bombarded demonstrators protesting the Shanghai killings, and the British joined in with machine guns. Student protest, already simmering in "an unexpected and vigorous patriotic protest against the meeting in Peking of the World Christian Student Federation" in which students in mission schools were accused of being half foreign or "foreign slaves," spread rapidly against all foreign schools.

Books and articles began to appear dealing with the problem of mission schools growing out of the rising spirit of nationalism, and Dr. Timothy Ting-fan Liu inaugurated his presidency of the China Christian Educational Association by suggesting that first needed was a recognition of the gravity of the problem coupled with an understanding of what the students thought and felt, and why. He believed the difficulties originated at least in part in Christian teachings that urged "independent thinking, encouraged interest in national salvation, in national welfare, and in practical citizenship," that "we owe these young leaders, full of initiative, often impulsive, the fullest sympathy."

Missionaries, under the same extraterritoriality that protected the police responsible for killing the Shanghai students, recognized that their acceptance of their governments' policies placed them at the center of the problem. They felt involved and responsible. My father took it upon himself to try to counteract some of the worst distortions of the story dominating the foreign press by publishing articles both in China and in America urging Americans to see what had happened through Chinese eyes and to work toward getting Washington to revise her treaties with China.

There was a growing missionary consensus to develop a group position and make it known. Those on Lushan, representing missionaries in Kiangsi, Kiangsu and Anhwei, appointed a committee, in which my father took a leading part, to draft a letter to the US Secretary of State, Frank B. Kellogg. In it they commended the proposed International Conference on Extraterritoriality, and urged that its scope be widened to include revision of unfair treaties with China, so that China could regain control of her own tariff, internal revenue and territory, controls essential to her sovereignty. The missionaries believed foreigners in China, missionaries especially, should come under Chinese authority, that the risks involved would be far outweighed by the goodwill generated. They took seriously the Methodist seminary quip that a preacher had to be ready at a moment's notice to preach, move — or die.

The letter to Secretary Kellogg was presented to the group for discussion on Lushan in early July, and at that same meeting it was decided a statement should also be made to their Chinese co-workers. Drafted and redrafted as ideas came in from absent members of the summer community, a proposal was finally laid before sixty missionaries crowding Beebe Hall on 23 August 1925. Forty-four remained to the end of that long evening of high excitement and signed the document which informed their Chinese friends that they had petitioned their government to remove all discriminations from treaties with China, affirmed that there "is no Christian justification for the aggressive, arrogant, and superior attitude which had characterized the dealings of many Westerners with Chinese," and confessed that often they themselves "had become unconsciously guilty of this attitude of superiority." It closed expressing confidence in the ability of missionaries and Chinese to work together.

Drought set in that summer of 1925, fierce fighting continued between warlords, villagers were terrorized, deserters roamed the countryside, the wounded piled up, protesters came inland from Shanghai, schools closed and churches were thrown into turmoil. About three-fourths of the Anhwei Methodist middle schools closed, most of the missionaries evacuated for a short time.

My father, bursting with questions as he tried to keep abreast of the confusing scene, felt increasingly miscast in his administrative role. He concluded he was better fit by temperament and training for seminary teaching, and that it was in the direction of self-determination for the Chinese Church that he wished to serve.

"I am still," he wrote to his bishop, L. J. Birney, "under the spell of that wonderful man of God, Dr. Albert C. Knudson. I should like to do for Chinese theologues what he did for me."

He was well aware the opportunities for seminary teaching in China were limited. Seminaries were few and were supported interdenominationally, which meant that Methodists were responsible for filling only a few positions. He knew he would be expected to sign conservative doctrinal statements to which he could not put his name.

Nevertheless, convinced that times and attitudes had to change and were changing, he believed there lay ahead of him a lifetime of work with Chinese theological students, for which his experience in his district gave him an excellent background in local realities. He snatched every possible moment for reading, studying, thinking, and asked Bishop

Birney to recommend him for a missionary fellowship at Union Theological Seminary during his furlough year.

As the end of my father's first term in China approached, many of the attitudes and ideas with which he had arrived had been badly shaken. But he looked to the future, both China's and his own, with typical optimism. He now had a wife and a three-year-old daughter, and the term had been financially as well as emotionally costly. As he assessed his expenditures, which each year exceeded his earnings and his indebtedness increased, he concluded, "But we feel no fear, the years are full of promise and in God is our trust. On $1,300 a year, whom else could we trust?"

My father at a "baby tower" where babies were left by parents who could not feed them. Most were girls as boys were more highly prized, as they still are today.

Helen Wolf

Paul G. Hayes

Nanking's city wall was the longest in the world, that of Paris second and Peking third. It took twenty-one years (1366-1386), 200,000 workmen to build, and was financed by rich Ming officials. Parts of the wall dated from the Eastern Han (212 AD). It was surrounded by a large moat with busy boat traffic. My parents walked its twenty-two mile circumference several times. Not foursquare as was usual, it undulated over and around hills. In 1980 about two-thirds were still standing.

Nanking's city wall and Purple Mountain seen through the arch of the Taoist Pink Temple. A magpie nest is in the foreground.

An avenue of stone animals and of civil and military officials led (and still leads) to the Nanking Ming tomb built 1381-1382 by the first Ming emperor, Hong Wu. Six paired animals sitting or kneeling, followed by a pair standing are followed by mythical animals, each with a mane and one horn on its head. Four tall majestic camels and four elephants with enormous heads are followed by four Chilin. These imaginary animals have scaled bodies, one horn on each head, deer hoofs and cow tails. Their meaning is not clear, but it was thought that a woman who succeeded in throwing a stone that stayed on the elephant's back would be granted her wish for a son. Here members of the Language School group get a close look at the camel. Always ready for a lark, Mother is seated in the center, in a dark skirt. It could be my father beside her, examining the carving, a typical thing for him to do, or perhaps he took this photo.

There are two dragon screens in the Imperial City within Peking. This one, where my parents posed in 1921, is probably the more famous Nine Dragon Screen built in 1417 to protect a temple no longer standing. Over fifteen feet high and eighty-seven long, it is made of glazed tiles in various colors. The nine dragons play with balls in the waves. You can see it today on the north side of Lake Peihai near the Ten Thousand Buddha Pavilion built by Chien Long for his mother's eightieth birthday.

Women flailing rice from its hulls.

Grain was ground by hand, sometimes powered by a donkey or a camel.

Women washed rice, vegetables and clothing in small ponds

Paul G. Hayes

Helen Wolf

My parents knew the word coolie meant bitter strength, but were unprepared for what those words actually meant. My father was struck by how impossible it might be to preach Christ's gospel of goodwill to the undernourished and overburdened.

Swept Up in the Revolution

ხOW COULÕ A SQUARE FIT INTO A CIRCLE,
ANÕ PEOPLE OF ÕIVERSE VIEWS
LIVE PEACEFULLY TOGETჩER?

— LI SAO (TჩირÕ CENTURY BC)

On that long day of 24 March 1927, when General Chiang Kai-shek's Northern Expedition reached Nanking, Edward James was searched to the skin and beaten by soldiers who looted his home, ripped out doors and windows, then swung a great sword over his head threatening to kill him unless he produced $400 in gold. Already robbed of all he owned, Dr. James was rescued by Chinese, some complete strangers, who literally put their bodies between him and the soldiers, then dug into their own pockets for the money demanded. They hid Dr. James under a pile of lumber when the soldiers left and brought him tea and rice until after dark when they led him to Bailie Hall at the University of Nanking. There all the missionaries were being gathered under protective custody after British and American warships had laid down a barrage around Socony Hill where the American Consul General, J.K. Davies, and a group of Westerners from the business community were under siege. Under protection of the barrage they escaped over Nanking's great wall and across the flats to the ships. The naval commanders then threatened to bombard the city if the missionaries were not given safe conduct out.

As we journeyed from Shanghai to New York the year before, my father was aware that he left behind an unstable political situation that could explode with painful effect on missionaries who in their persons, churches, schools and hospitals symbolized foreign encroachment on Chinese life. They could become targets for both Nationalists and Communists.

Chiang's Northern Expedition, long planned by Sun Yat-sen to rid China of warlords and unify the country, swept north from Canton to Hankow then east through the Yangtze Valley to contain the agricultural and industrial base around Shanghai. His troops, who were paid, bought their own food, slept in temples and generally treated the people in their path decently. Nanking expected the same.

What happened at Nanking, if noted at all in the histories, is compressed into one sentence: eight foreigners were killed before the British and American warships laid down a barrage so that other foreigners could escape under their fire.

Barely a footnote to Chinese history, the Nanking Incident was a time of anxiety, personal harm and loss for foreigners. As if it were not enough to have their homes ransacked once, to be stripped of possessions, manhandled and frightened by shooting, some families experienced this over and again, expecting each time to be killed, as each new group of marauding soldiers arrived. Many Chinese suffered equally brutal treatment, yet it was a time in which missionaries learned how completely they had been taken into the hearts of the Chinese, for both friends and many who were strangers came to their aid at personal risk.

Danger threatened as Chiang's armies approached Nanchang, some 500 miles to the west, where the Libby family left for Kiukiang by train. Cautioning the children to be quiet, Walter Libby silently handed Jim, Paul and Alice out a train window to Chinese waiting with outstretched arms below a darkened car. Pregnant with the twins, Lucile gathered up the three older children and continued the long hazardous journey to Nanking while Walter returned to the surgery at Nanchang Hospital where he treated Northern troops and put them out the back door as wounded Southern soldiers came in the front.

In Wuhu Robert Brown had the grim and lonely distinction to be the lone Methodist missionary at his post, the others evacuated to Nanking when Wuhu went over to Chiang. By staying he saved his staff from scattering and the hospital still under construction from looting. The two Methodist hospitals closest to Wuhu each lost equipment valued at $40,000.

Wuhu went over to the Canton-based revolutionaries relatively peacefully, but at Ichishan more than a hundred soldiers were in the compound, soldiers who kept their arms with them on the wards and threatened doctors and nurses who wouldn't do exactly as they wished. Chinese friends appealed to military authorities and "got better soldiers to surround the hospital and disarm the unruly men." Then the army pushed on toward Chinkiang and Nanking, leaving many wounded and chronically ill behind, adding to the mission's financial burdens, for they did not pay bills and had to be fed at a time when food was scarce.

In Chinkiang Duncan Dodd, then Methodist Mission treasurer, was hidden by Chinese friends as his home was looted of everything from piano to children's toys, doors and windows ripped out, floors and furniture chopped up for firewood, Mission records destroyed.

In Nanking Pearl Buck's family was hidden by Chinese in a hut eight by ten feet for thirteen hours as the three men, two women and three small children listened to shouts of the mob, watched flames from their home and from Nanking Seminary where Andrew Sydenstricker's work on translation of the Gospels into Chinese was destroyed.

At the University of Nanking Arthur J. Bowen, its president, was standing beside John Williams, its vice-president, when Dr. Williams was shot and killed. At the Ming Te School, Anna M. Jarvis disregarded American consul warnings to leave because Chinese women and children had brought their bedding to the school before the Southern soldiers arrived, feeling safer in the mission compound with the Chinese Red Cross flag flying over it, than they did in their own homes. But no one really expected violence. Chiang had promised to leave foreigners alone.

Shot twice, above one knee and through the abdomen, then left where she fell inside her front door, Anna Jarvis was hidden by students under a pile of straw in a shed throughout that long day. Feverish and sweating from her injuries, she lay listening to the looting, wondering when fire would be set to the school building or the shed in which she sheltered, while workmen who were complete strangers to her crept in with words of assurance and bowls of cooked rice and pickled cabbage, the food of the very poor, until dark when she was carried to Bailie Hall.

More than a hundred men, women and children whose persons and homes had been savaged, were gathered in Bailie Hall as rescue parties went out after the barrage and were given whispered directions by Chinese who knew where the foreigners were hidden. The next morning, stretched out on improvised beds, they listened as a list was read of those to work on food, sanitation and bedding committees and broke into laughter as they realized they had lost all else, but not committees.

Then Chinese began to arrive, most in tears; a coolie with a bucket of fresh milk, another carrying a huge Nationalist flag, with oranges and his last two dollars for the foreigners; Mr. Ma from the Industrial School with a load of towels, a laundryman with two huge baskets swung from his carrying pole filled with sheets and towels sent him that Monday. Students, teachers, servants, tradespeople, Christians and non-Christians, friends and strangers, brought food and clothing and offered to return to ransacked homes to search for valuables.

Under Nationalist troop conduct the missionaries were taken next morning to Hsiakuan, where launches transferred them to the warships. Outside the city they passed hordes of disarmed Northern prisoners, whose haggard, dirty, starved and hopeless faces were to haunt Anna Jarvis. The Socony Hill group had signaled the HMS *Emerald* and American destroyers *Nao* and *Preston* and clambered over the wall under the artillery fire laid down to protect them. Early next morning, after everyone was aboard, guns were raised again from the ships and turned on Hsiakuan in response to what appeared to be a threat from the Nationalists. But guns were lowered on both sides, and just after sunrise the ships raised anchor and made the 200 mile run to Shanghai in a record ten hours, forts along the way firing on them as they passed, but causing no damage.

This terrifying time led to serious conflicts of opinion as to what had actually happened, how serious the threat to their lives had been. Some felt sure the lives of their families had been saved by the bombardment, others insisted the soldiers were robbing and looting, not intending to kill, for they had it in their power to do so but generally held their fire. An eyewitness noted that Dr. Williams fell from what could have been an accidental shot among many fired to intimidate the group he was in. The Catholic fathers had fared far worse, seven of them killed, and the situation at Socony Hill was different because an American consulate guard had killed two Chinese soldiers. The foreigners' lives there were saved by the warships.

My father met missionaries as they returned to New York, sorted through oral and written testimonies and concluded that only the Hunanese soldiers were responsible for the violence. Triggering the event, he thought, may have been the common expectation of armies to loot coupled with Communist teachings of this particular regiment "to sweep like a hurricane the imperialists, the landlords and the local tyrants into their graves." It may have included an effort to discredit Chiang who had promised safety to the foreigners. Blame was eventually placed on one regiment of Hunanese troops trained under the Communists. On reaching Shanghai Chiang broke with the Communists in a savage campaign in which a number of Chinese Communist leaders were lost, Borodin and other commissars returned to Russia and the Chinese Communists were forced underground or into the countryside.

Distressed that after having developed strong opposition to gunboat diplomacy so many of his friends had felt it necessary to resort to navy protection, my father entered the debate with a number of published articles, one titled, "Vicarious Suffering at Nanking," by which he meant that the Nanking missionaries had suffered as representatives of the whole history of foreign wrongs in China. He was more convinced than ever that the unequal treaties should be abrogated, the unjust practices built up on them ended.

The Foreign Mission Conference of North America, an international and interdenominational group, appointed a committee to study the relationships between the various mission boards, their governments and the Chinese people. Their November 1927 report urged all boards, without delay, to ask their governments to withdraw all military forces from China and to hasten the abolition of extraterritoriality. They also urged speedy compliance of mission schools to register with the Nationalist government as demanded, and to grant Chinese Christians more voice in the control of mission funds and property.

The Methodist Board was slow to respond to this challenge, prompting a group of fourteen, including my father and called together by Boston University professor Dr. Harry F. Ward (who would be founder of the Methodist Federation for Social Action and chairman of the Civil Liberties Union) to try to stir both Board and US Government into action. The Board responded by dispatching a secretary to Foochow, Peking and Shanghai to consult with missionaries who promptly proposed far-reaching changes in Methodist practices. As a result, the 1928 General Conference revised objectives of Methodist missions in China to include Chinese principles of self-determination, self-propagation and self- government.

Wise boards scheduled regular furloughs, important years of refreshment, of study and travel and renewal of ties with families and friends. We had escaped the Nanking Incident when my parents' furlough fell due in 1926.

Using his Board allowance for passage direct to New York and arranging to pick up salary checks en route, my father booked us on a three-month trip from Shanghai to Port Said, across the Mediterranean, Italy, France and England to New York, family reunions, and a year when all three of us were at Columbia University. Mother was at Teachers College where I was also reluctantly admitted at the age of three to Horace Mann Kindergarten, while my father had been granted the Missionary Fellowship at Union Theological Seminary.

It was a stimulating year in which he grounded himself more thoroughly in New Testament studies, and in the history and culture of China under the guidance of Dr. Lewis Hodous, sinologist who doubled as Director of East Asian Studies at Columbia and at the Kennedy School of Missions in Hartford.

Of special influence on my father that year was Dr. Hu Shih, China's outstanding philosopher and statesman of the time, a visiting lecturer at Columbia on the Chinese literary revolution. Although Hu was not the first to advocate that China break away from the written use of the literary language which had not been on the tongues of the people for two thousand years, he was founder of the group that carried this movement to use the Chinese vernacular to national acceptance by writers, publishers and the literate public.

Chiang's Northern Expedition stopped all flow of missionaries to China for the balance of 1927, precluding our return, so my father decided to continue his studies with Dr. Hodous in Hartford, arranged to be summer preacher at Clinton-Westbrook and to switch to a charge nearer Hartford in the fall.

Charles Lindbergh was being cheered through the streets of New York as we set out by bus for Clinton, where my father was caught up in the Sacco-Vanzetti case receiving wide publicity that summer. That the

two men were about to be executed out of hysteria revealed a development in his country that alarmed him and implicated him because he
was expected to take "the best of our civilization to the Orient." What he
saw happening was not civilized, and he refused to be a "blind apologist
for things American." He preached on the imperative for the Church to
speak out against the death penalty in general as well as against this particular misdirection of justice, but never did learn the reaction of his congregation to this sermon, his last before moving to Hartford. Windsor
Locks Grace Methodist Church was his student appointment, and to
make the round trip each Sunday he bought a 1924 Chevrolet. Pauline
had an iron rod for a pedal, a hole in the floor that made winter travel
frosty, but she was a car, and with the help of a neighbor my father
learned to drive her.

This second year gave him more time to think about the message of
Christianity in the modern world and to track down more methodically
his position on war as he reexamined it in the light of the life of Jesus. It
gave him time to study the great philosophers of the Western world and
the teachings of the great philosophers of China. As though this did not
give him enough to think about, he had been reading what Methodist
writers had to say on theological themes, and they were not writing in
terms of the Articles of Religion adopted in 1784. They were thinking
about implications of their religion in the modern world, and what the
Articles said Methodists no longer believed. He began to examine all the
formal documents of his church and found many places where he
thought they could be updated.

Once more a pastor, he found it difficult to read reverently scriptures
designated for the day. "I said in my haste, all men are liars," hardly set
the tone for worship. In a church where he was guest speaker on China,
his host pastor was faced with the words, "Thou hast destroyed the
wicked. Thou hast rebuked the heathen. Thou hast put out their name
forever," to which the congregation responded, "The heathen are sunk
down in the pit that they made."

These and other readings from the Psalms hardly reflected the spirit
of Jesus and my father promptly wrote articles saying so that brought re-
sponses encouraging him to rewrite portions of the *Discipline,* and only
for lack of time did his enthusiastic revision of the voice of his church
come to a halt.

Having taken his doctoral examinations, and thinking he would have time to write his dissertation in China, my father boxed the papers and books he would need and prepared to return. One more year would have given him his doctorate, and Mother her BS. He did not realize he was heading back to seven years of administrative work more demanding than any he had known. Nor did he realize his outspoken attitudes following the Nanking Incident had been interpreted by some members of the Mission Board to mean he was unwilling to return to China unless the warships were removed from the Yangtze.

When this rumor reached Robert Brown in Wuhu, he wrote the Board an impassioned letter of support for his younger colleague, that he was sure this was not true, and that everyone on the field held Paul Hayes in high esteem, one Chinese worker of long experience regarding him as "the best missionary that had come to China in his time. . . they feel that he is scholarly, has broad sympathies and can see both sides of questions. He is also willing to be helpful and not dictatorial. This is the type of man we need in China now. . . ." The Finance Committee, then composed of seven Chinese and two foreigners, voted unanimously for his return.

As my parents packed they realized that only six months before, a great civil war had been in progress. "But revolutions," my father maintained, "are never permanent, and China's will come to an end." As he thought about the fifteen years it took America's few millions to set up representative government, he knew China's 450 million had made enormous progress in seventeen years. In contrast to China's huge potential for disaster, radical action and destruction had been relatively small, self-restraint relatively great. Anti-foreign outbreaks, he maintained, were superficial, temporary reactions against evils that needed correction. He believed that China's new leaders knew they needed Western trade and culture to reach their goals, that while the Soviet influence had been great it was temporary because China could use only a few details of the Soviet economic system, that China's ancient culture had a far greater influence than the temporary reaction against it. He believed the peasants to have finally wakened against the landlords and warlords and that the success of the revolution was a matter of time.

He saw real reasons to hope for restoration of international goodwill in the pledge of the Nationalist leaders to follow diplomatic procedures to secure redress for wrongs China had suffered from the West. Great Britain had already made concessions, and the United States maintained its historic friendship despite 1927 and was slowly moving toward equal treaties. And Japan had come to depend on China for raw materials and markets. "The new competition in the Far East is ostensibly goodwill toward China, and Japan will play the game," he hoped, then added, "in so far as self-interest will permit."

It was a family full of hope that headed west in Pauline in May 1928 for the three-month journey of 7,000 miles through twelve states where the Board had scheduled my parents to speak on China in various churches. We visited friends and relatives, historical sites and the natural wonders of America along the way to Seattle and the *Empress of Canada.*

Baggage strapped on the running boards and leveling off the back seat for me, Pauline served us capriciously but well, costing only 5-1/2 cents a mile, breaking a connecting rod, requiring several adjustments to the steering wheel and every 500 miles new spark plugs. Pauline took off on her own one day after we had stopped at a tourist home, but my father ran alongside and was able to jump in and bring her to a halt on the edge of a pond. She skidded through Kansas gumbo into a ditch, gasped for water climbing the Rockies and recovered her wind while I, with pole and bent pin, fished in the ditches. She passed and repassed an elderly lady driving an electric car so that to this day when I look across a map of the United States I see a small black car in endless transit, driver bolt upright, long thin face severe under an immense hat pinned in place with a veil. Pauline carried us safely to Seattle, where my father sold her for fifty dollars more than he had paid for her.

Howard A. Smith

Yangtze junk below our home on Ichishan

Howard A. Smith

Wuhu pagoda at the confluence of the Yangtze with a tributary. Standing for hundreds of years, it continues to welcome ships on the Yangtze to the ancient city of Wuhu.

On the Brink of the Thirties

IF YOU DO NOT TRAVEL, YOU WILL NOT REACH
YOUR DESTINATION; IF YOU DO NOT ACT,
YOU WILL NOT ACCOMPLISH ANYTHING.

— CHINESE SAYING

Wan sui! Wan wan sui!" Long live China! Ten thousand times ten thousand years! With the toast once reserved for emperors, the Japanese warship commander sprang to his feet amid shouts from all sides to toast Double Ten (10 October) 1928, the seventeenth anniversary of the founding of the Republic of China, at a feast given by the Anhwei Commissioner of Foreign Affairs for a hundred civil, military, business and missionary guests.

It was a night of high excitement, addresses by the commissioner and commanders of the Eleventh and Thirty-seventh Chinese armies followed by congratulations from commanders of the American and British warships in port. But my father, one of the guests, remembered that not long before similar toasts uttered in Korea by Koreans had cost them imprisonment and death at the hands of the Japanese. He remembered Japan's seizure of Shantung in 1914 followed by its Twenty-One Demands which touched off a spirit of Chinese nationalism. He remembered the 1919 Paris Peace Conference decision to leave Shantung to the Japanese, which cut short Chinese expectations for a chance at self-determination and set off bitter anti-Japanese demonstrations and boycotts known as the May Fourth Incident.

Such celebrations were held throughout China in 1928, celebrations at which the new flag, a white sun in its blue sky on a field of red, was raised over orators proclaiming "the downfall of selfish militarists and dirty politicians," heralding "a new government absolutely committed to the people's welfare." In truth, everyday life seemed to be returning to normal, the new Central Government was functioning better than many critics expected, and everyone hoped for justice and efficiency.

But the new government was still trying to find its way through an undercurrent of resentment on the part of those who had lost property or position or face during the revolution. Exorbitant taxes brought many to despair, while new officials who had once voiced high ideals were charged with graft and corruption and opponents were branded "communists" and ruthlessly destroyed. The long-heralded New China still had a tough road to travel.

We had been back in Wuhu about ten days before Double Ten, and the uncertainty of the times reached down to my five-year-old level, although I would not know for many years that my parents had expected to find our home in ruins and looted.

But when our steamer docked and we rode rickshaws back to Ichishan, there was the new hospital, apparently unharmed, there was our house, still standing. Climbing the rickety wooden outside stairway to our second floor storeroom, we found books and household possessions intact. My father was so thankful that he sent a list of his books to the University of Nanking, which had lost much of its library, followed by a hundred volumes of their choice.

Our return coincided with Annual Conference, which was being held in Wuhu that year. Someone was needed to reopen the work in Chinkiang, and my father was appointed its district evangelist, assistant to the Chinese district superintendent. We went down river soon after Double Ten and were in Chinkiang until the end of May 1929.

A port on the south bank of the Yangtze not far from Nanking, Chinkiang, meaning "guard the river," is at the junction of the Yangtze and the Grand Canal, a strategic location that caused it to be much fought over through its long history. Reports from Chinkiang of brisk trade in silk, vinegar, pickled vegetables, in bean-cakes, sesame seed and ground nuts, go back to ancient history, and Marco Polo commented on its rich merchants, plentiful game and abundant supplies of all kinds. Although the city boasts a fine harbor, its potential for trade was never fully realized after the opening of the Shanghai to Nanking and the Tientsin to Pukow railway lines.

Chinkiang had often known troubled times. In recent history it was captured by the British in 1842, the Taiping rebels held it from 1853 to 1857, then in 1858 the Treaty of Tientsin opened it to foreign trade. In 1889 a mob destroyed half the foreign buildings in the city, and in 1927 foreign property was again the target for anger and frustration with the Western presence.

When we reached Chinkiang, the first foreigners to return after 1927, disbanded soldiers still roamed the countryside raiding cities and villages under such names as Big Sword, Big Knife or Yellow Flag. They killed people indiscriminately, occupied and damaged churches and other mission property. Even in Nanking, the capital only a few miles away, the large Kuilan Church was continuously occupied, and Nanking Seminary buildings were saved only by renting them to the government.

When Chiang Kai-shek had reached Nanking in 1927, he established a one-party Kuomintang, Nationalist Government, which claimed to govern all of China. But there was dissension within the Kuomintang, and three powerful leaders still opposed him, Wang Ching-wei in Hankow, and the warlords Feng Y-hsiang in Peking and Chang Tso-lin who went his own way in Manchuria.

Then Chiang made a bold, but traditional move. He resigned.

He went to Japan, ostensibly to seek solitude, but actually to press his courtship of Soong Mei-ling, daughter of Charles Soong who was a Christian as well as a wealthy manufacturer and publisher. Chiang was sure that to be identified with this powerful family would be a great asset. Mei-ling as his wife, educated in the United States, would be his eyes, ears and sometimes his voice in dealing with the Western powers.

Their marriage, 1 December 1927, helped swell the popular clamor for Chiang's return to office to deal with party dissension and renewed war with the Communists. The government in his absence had relaxed controls, bandit outrages had increased, students demanded war, the Japanese consolidated gains in Manchuria. Chiang had demonstrated how necessary he was to national success, and the Central Committee of the Kuomintang hastily met and restored him to his post as Commander-in-Chief. In 1928 he resumed the Northern Campaign and got the support of all who opposed him except for Chang Tso-lin in Manchuria. But it was only on paper he had united the country.

In Chinkiang we settled into makeshift arrangements in the Olivet Girls High School where Mother taught English, while my father, with responsibility to oversee restoration of two wrecked mission homes, reached them by shortcuts over dikes and around paddy fields. He taught Bible classes in two city churches and four in the countryside, and took part in a forty-town evangelistic campaign organized in response to an upsurge of interest in Christianity following 1927. Daily travel around the district made him uncomfortably aware of the lawlessness that had taken over the countryside, the roving gangs of bandits evolving as huge armies disbanded.

In those Chinkiang days, most of what impressed itself on me was close to the ground where I was. An image of feet dominates my memories, feet coming and going at a pace out of tempo with a country tuned to the rhythm of walking, where Chinese seldom went far from their places of birth but where missionaries bustled about.

Every mission home was a rest stop for others, and they shared what they had: food, beds, ideas, news. Their chief recreation, talk, frequently gave way to argument over scripture, creating a sometimes embattled climate through which my father's voice would sound, clear, level, reasonable, conciliatory. So reasonable, indeed, that as I grew older and found myself trying to express ideas that ran counter to his, I could understand the distress of those who found it hard to argue with him and retreated into anger.

The long, long prayers before breakfast when the older generation was present at our table, made me shift from foot to foot behind my chair as I heard in those prayers veiled criticisms of my father by the tough, stern, white-haired men who would eventually prevail. Caught in tensions I did not understand, I found a way of escape one dinner through the spinach on my plate. The voices washed over me as I examined the long, tender green arms I had seen opened to the same sun that warmed me, imagined their white toes squishing as mine did in brown mud. This was a living creature I was to chew and swallow.

The idea shot through me exactly as did the electricity when Dottie and I took one another's dare to poke a finger into an electric socket. Just as suddenly came the return charge: the spinach was now me, I the spinach. I had found an escape from the voices of barely restrained passion. When they rose, I concentrated on identifying with the egg in my bowl, the chicken between my chopsticks, with the fish that lay whole, head to tail in golden-brown sweet/sour sauce, its flesh white and sweet for our needs, the "bounty for which we give thanks, O Lord."

A whole new dimension was opened to me, one that went beyond food to include all that lived: the dusty viper in the bamboo thickets, the praying mantis on a spray of wisteria, the scrawny *wonks* (mongrels) and cats, the water buffaloes and ducks and geese. Why did grownups get so excited when it was all so simple; they said it themselves in church: you love God, and you love others (the *wonks* and fish and spinach were others, too), and you don't forget to love yourself.

Our few months in Chinkiang are for me a montage of our canary, first of a long line of golden singers, who surveyed our Easter breakfast table and then laid an egg. Of my amah snatching up a giant centipede with a pair of tongs from across my instep, then thrusting it into the stove where its sizzling stilled my howls, shocked me into an anguish for all suffering crawling creatures. Of Pearl Buck's childhood home near ours, ugly and stiff as mission homes were, too large, but with a fragrant garden gone to tangle and a white rose climbing over a broken verandah. Of school cisterns where reflections of the night sky held me spellbound until examination time when I looked down on the bloated body of a student who had given way under family pressures to succeed. Of bats with a wingspread of sixteen inches or more flapping through our dining room curtains chased by our cook with a broom. Of the brown *wonk* frothing at his mouth that streaked by me one Sunday after church as the adults stood talking in the dusty road, but turned his head slightly the other way and bit an elderly missionary, dooming him to a trip to Shanghai and painful rabies injections. Death from rabies was common then. Caught by the police at our gatehouse, the *wonk* was consumed as I watched and wondered.

While we were in Chinkiang, my father continued to support efforts to get the United States to abolish extraterritoriality. A petition, formulated and agreed to by the International Missionary Council, was sent to missionaries in China for endorsement or changes, then presented to the US government in April 1929. My father worked hard to get the document to reflect some of his convictions, and the Methodists in Central

China finally approved it with additional resolutions that dispensed with gunboat protection and insisted mission boards should not demand damages for injuries to property or individuals in 1927, then added a request that their government expect from the Chinese only such rights and privileges and courtesies as should prevail between all nations. This was their expression of confidence that China was working out, slowly and painfully, a new system of justice and protection for all, including her guests from foreign lands.

My parents were enthusiastic in their support of the document, knowing they might have to stand by their convictions with their lives, but choosing to put their trust in New China. They were unaware that serious rumors were already spreading through the city, rumors that anti-foreign trouble would erupt on Lunar New Year in 1929, when large crowds would gather at the temple grounds not far from our compound. When they heard the whispers, they shipped their books to Shanghai, then packed one suitcase to take along should we need to seek protection with Chinese friends. Our servants kept watch throughout the festival, no anti-foreign agitation developed and the crisis passed.

That summer of 1929 on Lushan my father's spirits sank. He was thirty-nine. With six years' graduate work in Biblical studies, philosophy and theology, he was still saddled with administration and bookkeeping for the Central China Conference. He had again been made an officer of the Kuling Sanitarium, with more than twenty houses that had stood empty during 1927 and 1928 to put into order, walks, drains and swimming pool to repair. Loaded with frustrations, he was under siege from his own feelings as well as from missionaries who opposed his theology, and some of his Chinese co-workers were just as difficult. Time and again, when my father had to be gone for days, his secretary/teacher would plod to our house each morning and sit silently contemplating between puffs on his pipe. On my father's return there would emerge the subtle Chinese resistance to the foreign presence, when he was so sorry, he always had a grandmother, cousin or aunt who had just died, and would be absent a week when the desk was piled highest with correspondence, much of it in Chinese.

My father's temper, which I felt could be as strong as my own, turned in on himself and emerged in raging headaches that lasted for days, and in a series of other minor but persistent ailments. Only once, when I was some years older, did I experience the full force of that temper. My mind was slow and dreamy and came to a standstill before the wonders of arithmetic. Exasperated, my mother gave up trying to explain long division and turned me over to my father whose patience also let go. Later, he asked my pardon.

He continued to prepare himself to work with educated Chinese influenced by Confucianism, Buddhism, Taoism and Mohammedanism, but his immediate church members were shopkeepers, laborers and farmers whose children wore silver amulets about their necks to guard them from evil, whose wives tossed coins to the tops of stone animals with prayers to be given sons, who deflected evil spirits from their homes with spirit screens. Our neighbors in Chinkiang wakened us one night as they beat drums, banged metal and wood, explained by our cook: they had dealt with the well-known wonder in the sky, the devouring of the moon by the heavenly dog. By experience they knew the dog would be frightened by their noise and regurgitate the moon. It always worked. Unless there was some drastic change, my father realized, he would have to abandon his goal and find some way to reach his neighbors on the street.

Black Friday in America, 24 October 1929, went unremarked among missionaries, events in China obscuring this turn in history, its meaning for missions emerging only as the months passed. We were back in Wuhu, my father again district evangelist, assistant to the Chinese district superintendent. In the absence of Robert Brown on furlough, he was also appointed supervisor of the hospital buildings and grounds, with oversight of the office staff, boiler-room engineer, carpenter, and the many laborers whose daily tasks kept the hospital running smoothly.

I was aware of my father's leaden spirit as he set off mornings for his hospital office, but not of its cause. I was aware of the lift in him when he returned to settle down at his typewriter to carry on extensive correspondence with Upton Sinclair, who compelled him to "scrutinize my most precious beliefs, to criticize my deepest motives, and to adopt an objective and impartial attitude toward the social structure in which I am involved;" with Hu Shih and other Chinese scholars and Chinese Christian leaders as he probed to understand their attitudes; and with Frank Rawlinson, editor of *The Chinese Recorder*, the Protestant missionary journal published from 1868 to 1941, who opened to him its pages for articles and book reviews.

He went about with a preoccupied air. "Watch out! Here comes Hayes!" was apt to be the warning during breaks in conferences, in steamer saloons, along the mountain paths of Lushan, wherever he strode along in thought, his ears standing out "like billboards" said Mother, ready to buttonhole those he met with what was uppermost in his mind.

Invisible to me was the tremendous amount of work he put into understanding the social and political scenes both in China and America, the preparations he made to work with Chinese Christian leaders.

More visible were outward events. My world now included visits with Hyla Doc and Grandma Watters, Brownie and other adults, visits they received with courtesy and stories of their own childhoods. Soon I was also exploring the hospital. One day I saw the arrival of a long line of Japanese sailors carrying stretchers, but didn't understand the tension among the Chinese generated by their appearance. My father arrived at the emergency entrance on the run, having looked out his office window and noted with surprise a Japanese gunboat anchored off Ichishan, the line of crewmen headed our way. He summoned doctors and nurses to tend to the injured, who had been unloading cargo from a Japanese ship when a walkway collapsed, and was pleased that the Chinese staff, despite apprehensions, gave them the same kind of care they would have given their own countrymen.

Construction of the new hospital had brought other changes to Ichishan. As part of the project a new wall was being built, for the old wall Edgerton Hart had pleaded for had deteriorated badly, leaving the grounds open to visits from poor neighbors who helped themselves to everything they could carry off. At the time of the Brown's furlough, about a thousand feet of the new wall remained to be completed. Shortly before he left, Robert Brown entertained Chiang Kai-shek, who was at the start of his own decade of reconstruction and interested in such projects. I met the two men on the hospital steps as they walked and talked, the slim, intense, disciplined figure of the General ramrod straight in his uniform topped by the cape that was his trademark.

Robert Brown apologized for the appearance of the dilapidated gatehouse, and the General made a handsome gift to the project, which attracted contributions from other Chinese leaders, so that my father had the resources with which to finish the wall and to construct a fine gatehouse. Every week it was his task to settle accounts with the stone contractor. He found it complicated to figure the footage, but when he asked the *laopan* for his figures, they were invariably close to his own. He never saw the contractor doing any figuring, but the elderly man would stand with hands in his sleeves, a flicker of amusement in his eyes as he noted my father's curiosity, and acknowledge, *wo tsai tu-tzu li suan-i-suan*, I figure it in my belly. My father enjoyed working with men of real craftsmanship, and was convinced that a China based on the capabilities of many such men could not help but take her rightful place in the modern world.

Water, how to get it and clean it up, was always a major problem. The hospital's source was still the Yangtze, dirtied with over a thousand miles of surface runoff and the refuse of scores of cities. An electric pump had replaced the lines of coolies with buckets, which lifted the coffee-with-cream colored water into settling beds under the hospital roof, then by gravity reached all medical services and accessory buildings. During a storm, lightning knocked out its motor and once more lines of coolies moved up and down the hill behind our house and out through the Water Gate to the river. My father and Lao Wang the engineer went to the local light plant where they found an old motor, usable after some repairs, and the coolies melted back into the countryside.

Those first years in the new hospital were years of organization and growth in which the staff developed into a team able to work effectively together. Suddenly Western medicine was not only acceptable but popular, and there were ten qualified doctors in private practice in the city to whom the hospital gave every assistance possible. More problematic were the more than one hundred doctors of Western medicine whose qualifications included those of one former coolie who had scrubbed the hospital floors and advertised himself as trained at Wuhu hospital, and another who had "poured water over the hands of the foreign doctors," which was how the surgeons scrubbed up.

Christmas 1929 was a beautiful Christmas, our first with snow. It melted rapidly, but not before Dottie and I had a snowball fight and slid down the hill on a hastily constructed sled never used again. I was six years old and could see that my mother stood knee-deep in red tissue paper (dipped in pig's blood for color and always smelled like bacon) as she wrapped gifts for all the Chinese children on the hill, at least sixty patients, twenty-five nurses, thirty coolies and thirty hospital staff members. Red, the color of joy in China, where brides were dressed in red, was always used to wrap gifts, called *hung pao,* red package.

Two Shanghai American School girls whose parents lived in Fukien and Szechuan, too far for them to return home for the holidays, arrived in a flurry of high spirits and without boots or gloves. They kept our hand-cranked victrola churning out popular songs, trundled me by rickshaw to Asiatic Petroleum Company and other Christmas parties, leaned out the window Christmas Eve at midnight with me to listen to the nurses caroling. I was glad of their no-nonsense and cheerful company, especially after the Christmas Eve play at the hospital where staff enacted Dickens' *Christmas Carol* in inimitable Chinese fashion, the Ghost of Christmas Past grotesquely masked, robed in crimson and gold. He clanked chains fastened to his ankles as he strode across the chapel stage to stare directly down at me, or so I thought, and although I knew this was pretend, for me there stood Evil incarnate, its great eye pinning my terrified spirit to the floor where I had flung myself in fright.

After that the annual Christmas pageant was the nativity scene, sweet, tender, innocuous, in which I was expected to take part. I never made it beyond shepherd, but preferred the straw and shadows, enjoyed the goats substituted for sheep and wandered through my part wrapped in a sheet, head swathed in a towel, a cane crooked around the neck of the most obstreperous Tagenburg goat, Rosemary, to keep her from charging the kings as they stumbled in their bedspreads trying to look learned and impressive.

Before breakfast Christmas morning, as we gathered around our tree (made from one tall plank with arborvitae branches stuck into holes drilled along its sides so that the finished product resembled a tree without our having had to cut down a live one), its branches hung with garlands of silver and gold tinsel and glittering balls, presents heaped around its foot, servants, guests and family listened as my father read the Christmas story and gave thanks for the bounties of our lives. Then he gave the servants their red packages of money, socks and rubbers before distributing our own gifts, best of all for me a small, brown wriggly puppy with a black tongue and curly tail that had been left at the gatehouse the night before by Christian Missionary Alliance friends who had heard of my longing and were unaware of my parents' distaste for animals. Peter, rocked in my arms throughout that beautiful day and named before we learned her sex, entered my heart forever while her fleas took over the rest of me. After a good scrub for both of us, she earned the right to stay by sleeping quietly alone in the hall outside our doors.

The holiday spirit rolled through a week studded with Harold Lloyd films at the hospital, a chicken dinner for fourteen guests put on by my mother, with guessing games and shadow plays.

The valuable essential my mother brought to her serious husband and to both the foreign and Chinese communities, was her gaiety, a splendid tonic in this often grim world. How she loved a good time, and recreated for her new friends the fun her large family had known. She worked hard at her jobs as missionary wife and teacher, but perhaps her finest gifts came alive as the laughing, slender woman in a blue silk gown that matched her eyes and swirled around her ankles, danced through our drafty old Wuhu house reveling in her parties: rook parties, dinner parties, knitting parties at which the British sailors won all the prizes; birthday parties, farewell parties, Fourth of July parties; Thanksgiving, Christmas and Easter dinners; even backwards parties when guests arrived through the kitchen wearing their clothes buttoned on backwards to start dinner with pineapple upside-down cake and end with soup. My bedroom over the living room had a round hole cut through the floor for a pipe that in severe winters connected a second stove downstairs with a heating drum above. Most of the year it was a peephole into the adult world for me, a conveyor for messages on paper wads dropped into teacups below.

Preferring worn denim and tattered sneakers to pretty dresses, absorbed in stones, shells, twigs and insects stuffed into my pockets, I found the children's parties that meant so much to my mother a trial. Invariably I did the wrong thing: stuffed sticky sweets into the large handkerchief pocket sewn onto my drawers because I did not know what else to do with candy too sweet for my taste, backed into corners at game time, totally uninterested in winning a thing. At a Standard Oil children's party I was given a chocolate for the first time and, finding it unpalatable, fed it to the massive Great Dane who sensed which way the wind blew from across the room and beat my mother to it.

Basically timid (when my father was away Mother kept a bottle of ammonia handy by her bed, ready to hurl at intruders, but never had to use it), when cornered Mother fought back. Her umbrella, always with her as protection from rain or sun, was brandished when one of our suitcases was snatched from the deck of a Yangtze steamer. She got it back. Again, when she and I were walking a lonely road and were pushed against a wall by boys on water buffaloes demanding money, the umbrella came out. They retreated, as frightened as I was by the possibility she might use it. From the end of her bed she shook it at large rats invariably attracted by food gathered into our bedroom at night, when my father was absent, to keep it from being stolen.

Nor was she afraid to appear ridiculous. When she wondered how coolies descended Lushan, the mountain where we spent our summers, with so much more ease than she did, she imitated their toes-out, bent-knees jog, then, unable to straighten, walked around the steamer in her coolie crouch. When Hyla Doc wondered aloud what it felt like to pull a rickshaw, she and my mother took turns pulling each other down Ta malu. Mother refused to help Hyla Doc pluck tail hairs from the handsome horses tethered at the *yamen* to use for sutures, but that was not because she was afraid of appearing ridiculous but because she had been nipped by a horse as a girl when she drove a team delivering groceries for an older brother.

Mother taught English to student nurses, whose text books had not yet been translated into Chinese, and Chinese characters to neighborhood women who loved to come to our home for tea. Mother opened a shelter for unwanted infant girls who escaped death when placed by poor parents in a hole in the wall, which became the name of the shelter. She excused me from class the mornings Hyla Doc had surgery scheduled which I wanted to see, gallantly listened to my lunch-time descriptions of how Hyla Doc had sawed through a bone or dug out a bullet, although they turned her faint. But she had me prepared to enter public schools in America a year beyond my grade.

In China Mother sat in a welter of lists delegating tasks for the four servants, lists for the cook in a household where those at our table varied each day from three to a dozen, lists for my father to take to Shanghai for the monthly supplies that had to be tediously and fairly divided between the foreign households, even the oleo from Australia that melted into its rice-hull packing and had to be heated and strained.

Mother had the ability to get up and go, to take delight in the moment, to make something happen, and how she loved the strings of firecrackers set off on either side of the compound gate that welcomed us home from summers on Lushan. "Let's pretend!" tumbled cheerfully in the air as she rooted out bags of old laces and clothes for dress-up on rainy days.

Pretense and theater, she loved them both, and so did I, and found them when I slipped out the hospital gate to join crowds gathered about traveling musicians, tightrope walkers, jugglers, skit players. With everyone's attention riveted on the performance, we laughed and spit together, cracked watermelon seeds, chewed water chestnuts and sesame candies. For years I expected to grow up to be a tightrope walker, balancing my bamboo pole above the heads of a crowd.

Famine and flood might be a hairsbreadth away, but showmanship among the Chinese took precedence: the Dragon Boat races on the Yangtze during Spring Festival, firecrackers for every occasion, always a band of flutes and horns at the head of a funeral procession with room for one small foreign devil to march alongside singing, "Mine eyes have seen the glory of the coming of the Lord. . ."

The dramatic touch was everywhere. "In the presence of you and you and you," would intone my favorite rickshaw puller, poorest of the poor in this destitute land, and leap to his feet addressing his fellow pullers as they squatted in the dirt road beside the gate, dressed in mantles made from banana tree fibers and straw against wind and rain, ragged pants and little else, likely to make the announcement he was ready to go home. It was usual to speak of getting out of a bad situation as having got off the stage with credit, or that retirement from the stage was not so good, linking daily life closely with images from the theater. Theater, the pretense through which the ironic and the ridiculous receive full play, came as second nature to a people who lived on the brink of disaster, a bit of fun or swagger the lifeline to hope.

In the bright light of day I enjoyed the jokes and the crowds, the ad libs. There would be a good-natured assessment of performers, and what counted was aptness and success of improvisation. But there were times, especially at night, when I sensed a difficulty in distinguishing what was happening out in the world, what I was supposed to be seeing or thinking or feeling from what it was I saw and thought and felt.

At night came a recurring nightmare in which a double row of foreigners came toward me, rolling slowly along as though standing on a giant roller coaster. As they approached, each familiar face disappeared behind a wand with a painted face on it, and a huge voice boomed out of the darkness behind them. "Lovest thou me?" it would question, the reassuring faces of family and friends hidden behind the painted smiles so that I was left alone, vulnerable, unshielded, to meet this powerful voice.

"How can I love you if I don't know you?" I would quaver, although it seemed imperative to answer "Yes."

I thought the voice belonged to someone I was supposed to know named Jesus. I had been taught to sing, "Jesus loves me this I know. . ." my voice trailing off as I tried to think who this Jesus might be, for I was told he had died for me, which made me shudder, for I had seen people drowned, starved, beheaded, and I didn't want that to happen because of me. The dream always dissolved inconclusively, but returned, and would not let me alone.

When I was small, I have been told, I would rock my Paopei, my doll named Precious, singing to her, "Jesus loves me. . ." but I have no memory of it, while I do remember Paopei with a web of fine cracks for her face, so precious that she went everywhere with me, falling as I fell, and often on her own. The loss of Paopei, left behind when we first went to America when I was three, was linked with the loss of my amah into whose arms I had hurled myself, whose arms caught me up from every imminent disaster, whose arms soothed and cradled me through my infancy so that while to this day I have no image of her face, I would instantly recognize her touch should her arms tighten around me, recognize her voice in my ear.

The Chinese world of my amah's hug and the bustling missionary world, were not the whole of it for me. There was also the world of the menacing black stag beetles, the glorious azure-winged dragonflies, the imperial centipedes, sometimes twelve inches of black segmented body bracketed with bright red head and tail, underpinned by rows of sharp yellow feet. There were the surprisingly raspy young garter snakes and the big black racers and the delicate light green bamboo vipers. There were the chattering flocks of black mynahs and the lone cuckoo that drove us mad in the heat with its interminable repetition, *"Ko mai, ch'a ho,"* cut the wheat, plant the rice. There were the dogs and cats, buffaloes, goats and horses that stepped in and out of my life who were individuals that happened to come in shapes that differed from mine. I touched and smelled and cherished the small world about me and kept track of the tragedies there, mourning my losses. When I lifted my eyes to the world of men, the thrust of devastation was overwhelming.

As I look back I believe the flux and change of the natural world about me had none of the fixed moral scorekeeping of good and bad that characterized much of the mission world flooding over my head. These two worlds were constantly out of key with one another and with the Chinese world in which they were set.

Politely dressing up to me was a part of the effort to pretend that all was well when anyone could see that disaster walked everywhere, but no one would speak of it. It was many years before I learned that it is an American myth of long-standing that serious conflict between individuals as well as within and between societies is unnatural and unnecessary and can be resolved through relatively simple adjustments at no cost to anyone. I was baffled equally by the terrible results of conflicts that happened in the society around me, and by the never acknowledged conflict within our immediate family. Full of spirit and fun and genuine concern for the suffering around her, Mother was deeply dependent on the intellectual and practical man she had married. Feeling and intuition had little standing in the age of scientific enlightenment in which my parents had been nurtured, and they were unaware that conflict between different minds and personalities can be a challenge to growth rather than to combat. Foreign to them was the idea that those with differing strengths and weaknesses can learn from one another, adding to each life dimensions often painful always enriching, to acquire. Conflict there was, but not acknowledged; all that was unpleasant was carefully ignored.

In an effort to understand the game and play it, a fatigue crept over me that lasted a good part of my life. I learned to hug darkness and silence and aloneness, went underground in my feeling life as so many children do. Underground, a fertile, beautiful, wonderful adventure, sometimes frightening, was less so than to be on the outside where awful things happened to people. I learned to trust the inner life, to flow with it as it came, to believe that in movement and change were joy and growth. There I discovered light and dark to be two sides of one whole, met the *yin* and *yang* far from China with delighted recognition, finding in them the severed rabbit's head and the star flower in a red vase given to me by Hsiao Pao and Hsiao Shih.

On the brink of the Thirties the background to my life was disjointed and seething with the possibilities of explosion. We did not go to Lushan early in June 1930 as we usually did, for the political situation was volatile with the revolt of Yen Hsi-shan and Feng Y-hsiang in the north, "Communist outrages" reported from Honan, Hupeh and Kiangsi. We stayed down on the hot plains, each of us stepping into the bathtub whenever possible, my father typing at his desk with a handkerchief tied around his head to absorb the sweat, wiping drops from nose and elbows.

By November huge bands of Communists were moving across the countryside, rice shortages affected everyone, mission properties were being targeted by government agents. They required mission schools to register with the government, alter their curricula, and provide daily demonstrations in honor of Sun Yat-sen, which some missionaries interpreted as participating in ancestor-worship. At the University of Nanking the colleges of Arts and Sciences were required to become two separate schools, its Department of Religion was closed down and the Student Christian Association disbanded.

In December General Chiang Kai-shek was baptized in Shanghai, which brought some hope that sallies against missions might lessen, and indeed, by July 1931 the Nanking government issued a proclamation guaranteeing freedom of worship and relaxed its attitudes.

It was more than a year since Black Friday, a year that had turned black indeed for missions; the Methodist Board alone reported a shortage of $200,000. In Bulgaria all Methodists were urged to unite with the Congregationalists, in Burma with the Baptists, in France and Italy with other Protestant groups. Work in Germany, Sweden, Norway, Denmark was pushed toward self-support, the Swiss were asked to take on the American mission in Yugoslavia, Mexican Methodists to take over work in Costa Rica. Work among Muslims in North Africa was reduced to almost nothing, while in China the South Fukien mission was closed outright. The one bright note that my father could discern lay in the steadily increasing proportion of Chinese to missionaries in positions of leadership.

At home we joined the Great Depression by putting together jigsaw puzzles, all the rage in Depression America and sent us by Mother's family, and by eating only Chinese food. This was a fine improvement over foreign food, I thought, except that there were no more saltines or marshmallows.

Paul G. Hayes

Ru Ming, Buddhist monk on Silver Island in the Yangtze off Chinkiang, who became good friends with my father.

Ichishan, the mission hill crowned with the hospital, from the Yangtze in the 1930s. Our house is lowest on the hill, the Brown's between ours and that of Hyla Watters nearest the hospital.

Launch at Wuhu bund, often used by my father on trips up and down river to visit village churches. When passengers were excited or panicked, they tended to rush to one side, threatening to overturn the launch. My father thought perhaps he should learn to swim, but never was able to, despite much thrashing about in the Kuling pool.

Paul G. Hayes

A surgical patient of Dr. Watters' who had had a piece of diseased bone removed from her shin, ready to return to her job of loading coal on the Japanese freighter at the Wuhu bund.

Howard A. Smith

Tieh fantze, the iron dispensary in Wuhu. Hot in summer, cold in winter, it was still of great value in treating people uneasy about going to the hospital or found it too far off. It was located on Jing Hu, Mirror Lake. In 1980 I visited an art gallery on this site.

Howard A. Smith

Junk off Ichishan. To my sorrow, long shots of The River from our hill are too faded to reproduce. It was a riveting, ever-changing panorama, this ancient super-highway: freighters from many nations, fishing junks, pirate junks, sampan ferries to the far shore, rafts made of lumber to be sold downstream, sampans herding ducks to market; British, Japanese and Chinese steamers, some still with paddle-wheels; small round tubs paddled by beggar women besieging the steamers. And there were the warships of several nations, too many of our favorites sunk during World War II: shallow-draught gunboats, cruisers, destroyers, even the rare passing of a stately battleship. For a few years the *Villalobos* chugged by. Built in Hong Kong for Spain in 1896, she was captured in the Spanish-American War and re-commissioned in the US Navy. She was the semi-fictional USS *San Pablo* in Richard McKenna's book, *The Sand Pebbles,* on which a movie was based. In 1928 she was sunk in target practice.

Lewis L. Gilbert

The Thousand Steps on the ascent of Lushan, between The Ford and Crescent Moon Ditch. Too steep for chair-carriers, this was where children, pregnant women and amahs with bound feet had to make it on their own.

River and Mountain

... I CLIMB TO THE TOP, I SURVEY THE WHOLE WORLD.
I SEE THE LONG RIVER THAT RUNS BEYOND RETURN,
YELLOW CLOUDS THAT HAVE DRIVEN HUNDREDS OF MILES
AND A SNOWPEAK WHITELY CIRCLED BY THE SWIRL
OF A NINEFOLD STREAM.*
AND SO I AM SINGING A SONG OF LU MOUNTAIN,
A SONG THAT IS BORN OF THE BREATH OF LU MOUNTAIN...

— LI PO (701-762)

The Yangtze was a focus for all of us, Chinese and foreigner alike. Our eyes turned to it instinctively many times each day as we checked its traffic, its turbulence, its swollen or subsiding presence, its brown waves turned a smooth bronze under a full moon or whipped into cold gray waves by typhoon as sampans and junks were tossed about and sunk.

On awakening each morning I ran first to my bedroom windows open toward the river to watch the lovely slip of ghostly sails through billows of mist that lay over the water. As the light strengthened and the soft batting of the night shredded and disappeared, the full drama of the river emerged. My favorite place from which to watch that show was the long flight of stone steps leading up from the river to Ta ma-lu below our house. Common along waterways throughout China, such steps allowed

---

*   Chang Jiang, Long River, is the Chinese name for the Yangtze. Ninefold stream
     refers to the nine rivers that converge at Kiukiang at the foot of Lushan, giving
     the city her name.

for the enormous seasonal rise and fall of the river. There I could sit to one side as the water carriers swung up and down the steps, small launches puffed in and out of the bund beyond, flocks of ducks swam past to market and an occasional raft of logs came down mid-current, sampans, tubs, junks, gunboats and steamers all giving right of way to the huge unwieldy logs lashed together with a hut on top for the families of the men who leaned on its long sweep oar at the rear. On the rocks beyond me fishermen flung wide nets, while trackers, sometimes twenty or thirty bent double under the great hawser of a junk working upstream, came slowly into view, their feet slipping on wet rock, sweat rolling off backs, down legs with muscles straining over hardly more than bone. From time to time brown patches bobbed downstream into an eddy near the rock, close enough to reveal a dead pig or dog, once a gray putrid mass that was a man with arms and legs trussed behind him.

The *Poyang, Woosung, Chang-wo, Tuckwo,* beautiful names for the squat, shallow-draft steamers that steamed twice a week between Shanghai and Hankow at the height of the inter-port trade—from one treaty port to another in China's domestic commerce. They arrived on the river in the late nineteenth century in response to the need for shipping more secure and reliable than the Chinese, to usher in an American and British-led, Chinese-backed era of great steamboating on the Yangtze. Jardine, Matheson; Butterfield & Swire; Peninsular & Orient; China Merchants Steam Navigation Company; San Peh; and the Nishen Kisen Kaisha, the Japanese line: each had distinctive funnels, and it took no more than a glance to tell which was in port.

The Yangtze steamers, what a special world they were. There was the flurry of boarding from one of the hulks, literally old ship hulks used as wharves, although sometimes we boarded midstream, the steamer barely slowing as we clambered aboard from sampans rocking in the bow wave. Sweating, shouting coolies dumped our bags on deck, sailors hauled in ropes, the smell of tar and oil heavy in the air, Ningpoed (varnish made from poison sumac in the city of Ningpo) rails gleaming dark red and hot under our hands as we gripped them to watch the pull into the current. Then the bow wave arched coffee-colored as the great sidewheel or rear wheel churned in response to a series of bells.

I loved the small cabins with washstand that folded down, holes set into its gleaming wood frame for tooth-glasses and carafe, the small round porthole probably closed, its glass thick and wavy, needing a good tug on brass handles to get it open. Saloons were elegant with comfortable chairs and writing desks, tables for games, the dining tables set off with white linen and china, gleaming heavy-weight silver, under the punkahs.

Then there was the engine room, fascinating with its dials and pipes and the roar of boilers as sweaty stokers shoveled in coal to get up steam. Sometimes we were invited to visit the bridge and stand beside the steering wheel, perhaps four feet across, peering over it as it turned, to watch the river banks fall away until there was only the river and the steamer sailing through the night. Stretched out on the narrow bunks we would be lulled by the whir of a small fan high in one corner near the ceiling, turning its head slowly back and forth through the heat. In the morning low flat land would be visible far to each side.

My father used all the steamers on his trips to Nanking and Shanghai, trips that always combined mission business with shopping for the Wuhu foreign community and gave him a chance to stock his shelves with purchases from Shanghai's fine bookstores, and to indulge in his favorite pastime at the movies. He would tell us their stories which I carefully retold to an enthralled audience in the brick playhouse. In this way Dottie and I enjoyed George Arliss in *The Last Gentleman* and *The House of Rothschild,* Shirley Temple in *Now and Forever,* Leslie Howard in *The Scarlet Pimpernel. The Barretts of Wimpole Street, The Little Minister* and a dozen others made us film buffs forever.

We had a private family code that flourished as my father's steamer passed Ichishan and his white handkerchief waved from the deck in answer to a white towel from our verandah describing an up-and-down signal for "I," a circle for "love," and a horizontal for "you."

Sometimes all the cabins would be taken before he was able to board, and he would join a dozen others in the saloon where he would set up his typewriter at a writing table, then rent a deck chair for sleeping, or sometimes bed down on a couch. If he knew someone in a cabin he would have a place to shave and to store luggage and the sometimes strange supplies he was commissioned to deliver or purchase. In one letter he laconically noted that when his steamer reached Nanking he delivered the bed as requested. At other times he was entrusted with a child or gift, or to purchase garters, socks, Sterno, pumelos, oranges, shoe polish, a door spring, neat's foot oil, or to get a tennis racquet restrung, a watch repaired. We benefited in turn from this informal delivery service when my bike was brought from Shanghai, and the rugs now in my living room.

The warships on the river, daily and uneasy reminders to my father that he was personally involved in the war machinery of his own country, were an everyday part of our lives. A British gunboat was constantly tied up at the Butterfield hulk or anchored midstream, a Japanese gunboat along the Nishen anchorage. British, French, Japanese and American destroyers and gunboats patrolled the Yangtze, pointing up the domestic weakness of China and the imposition of foreign demands backed by naval power.

Whatever one believed about extraterritoriality (and most of the missionaries went on record in opposition to the system of foreigners being exempt from Chinese laws), or about the presence of foreign warships dominating Chinese waters ready to back up that unequal system, emotionally we were all tied to the men and officers who came from those ships to our homes for dinner and tennis, who gave us parties in return, allowed us children to romp through officers' quarters and to perch on the big guns for swivel rides. We were hugely indulged, stuffed ourselves on exotic hot dogs, snuggled down under steamer rugs to watch Laurel and Hardy, the Marx Brothers, Charlie Chaplin, building a mental image of America never to be matched in reality. I still have sailor hatbands for the USS *Edsall* and HMS *Cricket;* an old metal candy box decorated with hearts and flowers might yet be tucked under the floorboards in our Wuhu attic. One of our own, a son of our mission treasurer, was a lieutenant on the Yangtze Patrol flagship, USS *Luzon.* It was only years later when I read Richard McKenna's essay, *The Fiction of History,* and his novel, *The Sand Pebbles,* that I learned there had been friction between some missionaries and sailors.

We loved the HMS *Cricket, Aphis, Gannet, Gnat, Cockchafer* and *Scarab;* the *Ladybird* was a special favorite, as was the flagship of the British Yangtze Flotilla, HMS *Bee,* both shelled by the Japanese off Wuhu soon after the USS *Panay* was sunk below Wuhu 12 December 1937. We knew captains and crews of USS *Panay, Guam* and *Edsall,* ships companies of the *Oahu* and *Luzon,* all caged along with 11,000 other American sailors, soldiers, airmen and marines on The Rock after the fall of Corregidor, those of the *Edsall* lost with their ship, torpedoed by the Japanese. We learned to tell the ships apart from a distance by the shape and color of their funnels, the shape of bridge or aft structure, whether there was a crow's nest and where it was placed, idiosyncrasies of searchlight or signal flags. We learned from Hyla Doc how to signal in Morse, watched for the M flag to be raised, which meant a movie that night.

From Wuhu our world stretched upriver to the port of Kiukiang and inland about six miles across the plain to Lushan, the Hut Mountain, then up its craggy slopes to the small foreign settlement known as Kuling. How did it happen that we spent our summers on this mountain sacred to the Chinese? Among the foreigners serious illness and frequent deaths always increased during the heat and humidity. In 1894, when two strong young leaders of our Methodist Central China Mission succumbed, a Mr. E.S. Little followed charcoal makers up their trails in search of a summer retreat.

The beautiful valleys that he found, the streams, falls, pools and cliffs that had been celebrated by poets for centuries, were obviously healthy places of fresh air and clean water, and he urged acquisition of some land by the mission. Given the authority to negotiate for a parcel, he secured a forty-year rental from provincial officials. A lovely valley was set aside for the Methodists in compensation for time taken from his work to procure it, a valley without roads or houses, its upper limit marked by a fresh cold spring that poured from under a rock near the ridge.

My anticipation of our annual trip to Lushan peaked when the luggage was assembled—the clothing, food, kitchen equipment, baby carriage, *corries* (large rattan containers with covers) of bedding, the small brown Boston Bag known as the medicine bag—when servants and children were rounded up and everyone and everything loaded onto the upriver steamer for the overnight passage.

In Kiukiang, another ancient river port with a substantial mission history, we sometimes spent a second night in the guest house on a narrow street facing the river, usually a sleepless, hot night under dusty mosquito nets spent listening to the creak of junks along the shore, the clack of mah jong counters in the courtyard below accompanied by the murmur of voices. Children usually slept on the wide upper porch where the fragrance of the courtyard magnolia reached us, the grunt of a sleepy pig, thud of June bugs against a white arc light, the bark of a dog in the hills. Stifling nights, I remember my mother sitting by my bedside fan-ning me, neither of us able to sleep. Next morning brought the trip by bus, or sampan during flood, across the plain dotted with villages and temples to Lien Hua Tung where the bargaining started for coolies to carry luggage and sedan chairs up the mountain.

Although we traveled toward the mountain, it always seemed to me that the blur of gray peaks against the sky moved toward us, becoming a towering, heart-thumping presence. But it is not a high mountain, Lushan achieving its impressiveness by rising sheer from the Yangtze Valley floor, its small peaks of 4,500 feet presenting some of the grandest views in central China. During the last century it was still a wild, largely uninhabited place except for a few monks and charcoal makers and an occasional poet or painter.

Rising abruptly from the great plain, Lushan towers above the Yang-tze where it bends into Poyang Lake, the Big Orphan Island standing as she has for centuries within the main current of the river, the famous porcelain town of Chingtechen over there, the White Deer Grotto, founded a thousand years ago as a retreat for scholars, here under Lushan's shadow. Chu Hsi chose the grotto as the place to work on his commentaries on the classics in the twelfth century.

Steeped in legend and history, Lushan appeared in Chinese histories under many other names. Even the origin of Lushan, its popular name, is lost in antiquity. One of many stories has it that during the latter part of the Shang dynasty (1776[?]-1122 BC) two gods dwelt among the peaks for a time, and since wherever a god stays is his abode, his hut, or *lu*, the *shan*, mountain, which the gods honored with their visit, was called Lushan. The legendary Ch'in Shih-huang-ti, is said to have been the first emperor to personify and deify mountains, and to have named Lushan steward to the mountain then appointed Guardian God of the South. A later emperor promoted Lushan to this august position, and then Chong Chung (1068-1086 AD) of the Sung dynasty conferred even greater hon-ors by making the mountain a princedom and addressing it as the Guard-ian Prince of Destiny. Among Lushan's famous visitors is said to have been Ch'in Shih-huang-ti, who unified China for the first time in the third century BC, and who had the famous terra cotta army built to pro-tect his tomb. The T'ang (618-907) poets Li T'ai Po, Tu Fu and Po Yoh T'ien, were often drawn to its slopes and valleys. Their poems celebrating

Lushan were so widely read that they alone are sufficient to make the mountain sacred and immortal to the Chinese.

Mountains, the refuge of poets and artists whenever war threw China into turmoil, cradled some of her most spectacular artistic achievements. When the T'ang Dynasty fell in 907, the Northern Sung style of landscape painting emerged. When the Mongols dominated all of China in 1275, scholar-painters who fled to the mountains developed *hsieh-i*, a highly expressive, calligraphic style. With the ascendance to power of the Manchus in 1644, another brilliant age of Chinese painting was launched. Tao-chi (1641-ca. 1710), the marvelous watercolorist whose work is considered the most innovative of later Chinese painters, was born into a branch of the Ming imperial family. His unique style blossomed after he fled the Manchus. Surely the spirits of great artists and poets who mourned recurring foreign domination of their country and through meditation on their own and their society's failures reached deeper levels of truth to which they bore witness through their art, lingered along the Lushan trails to touch those of us who clambered along them so many years later.

As I look at my faded snapshots of Lushan, it is 1923. Paul and Helen Hayes, flat brown photographs, walk across the flat brown Yangtze plain through the heat toward the mountain. My mother, unsteady in her unaccustomed fullness (she was slight, vivacious, before she conceived me; what is she doing walking across a hot plain in China?) steps into a sedan chair, is hoisted to the shoulders of cheerful coolies and carried up the mountain to give birth to me in the Kuling Sanitarium. Tokyo rocks in its great earthquake. Sun Yat-sen is making an alliance with the Russians. Mao Tse-tung, a young man, is organizing peasants and workers in Hunan. We draw together, three brown faded photographs, vulnerable, desperately unaware, hopeful. In 1923 Lushan is a quiet sanctuary above the steaming valley where the summer mortality rate is very high.

The growing summer community on Lushan builds cool stone bungalows, and the death count among foreigners subsides. Unless they have been plowed under, thousands of missionary graves are still a part of the Chinese landscape. Men and women who went to China as my parents did, children born there as I was, often had no alternative but to lie down and die. Many from sickness. Many beaten to death or hacked to pieces with swords. The one word constant and unchanged in the 118 years of the Protestant missionary journal, *The Chinese Recorder,* is the word *martyr.*

For 1935, my last year in China, there is a list in the *Recorder* of fifty-four Protestant *Captives and Martyrs:* fifteen killed; one who died in captivity; others robbed and detained for a few hours or a day, some up to more than six months. Two were listed as "still held," four as "73 days besieged." Compared to the 1900 martyr list, this is a short one.

As China passed through the upheavals leading to her 1949 revolution, missionaries often took the brunt of frustration and anger. But it is, perhaps, in this experience of undeserved suffering that they came closest to sharing the everyday tragedy of Chinese life itself.

There are more graves now, on Lushan, of friends who made the hard, steep climb. Food, household equipment, baby carriage, all had to be loaded onto the backs of coolies; small children and pregnant women, amahs with bound feet, into sedan chairs. The rest of the caravans set out on foot. Hairpin turns in the narrow trail along cliff edges were frightening when one was young and alone in a chair swung out over valleys that could be glimpsed below on either side, but the carriers were sure of foot, and the magnificent peaks above and the plain spread out below made up for such moments. As soon as we were old enough, however, we took to our feet, glad to give up riding on the backs of others.

The first leg of the ascent wound through gentle foothills to the first long flight of stone steps where the climb began in earnest. At about eight hundred feet everyone took a deep breath of reviving mountain air near the Temple of the Iron Buddha set in a bamboo grove. Then the path wound along a deep gorge on the right where the stream rushed in long leaps over the rocks. Bamboo and fir were pretty much left behind here, and the *Shih Pa Wan,* The Eighteen Turns, took us on to the second rest hut at *Tou Li Shu,* Bamboo Hat Grove. From here the path became even steeper on another twenty minute climb to the third stop at *T'a Shui Ho,* The Ford, at about 1800 feet. Between *T'a Shui Ho* and the fourth stop at *Yueh Kung Ch'ien,* Crescent Moon Ditch, a steep ascent of a thousand steps was the most arduous part of the climb and too steep for sedan chairs to be carried. Everyone had to make it on his own. Above the Thousand Steps the valley widened and Kuling bungalows could be seen in the distance, still an hour's hike away along an almost level path that passed the turnoff to Lotus Valley where the narrow trail had been blasted out of the face of a steep cliff and an inscription on the rocks rising above the sheer drop read, "A delightful place for strolling about." An almost level path led on into the Gap, the business district, and where it crossed the stream a flight of another thousand stone steps led off to the right through *Chien Tao Hsia*, Scissors Ravine, to the Chinese village.

By June, when we usually reached the mountains, the spring hillsides ablaze with pink, magenta, deep red and orange azaleas, had faded. Our paths were edged with daisies, coreopsis and cosmos, the stark windswept crags gave way to grassy meadows aflame with tiger lilies; white and pink roses and fragrant honeysuckle swept across open spaces. In my garden today blooms a blackberry lily from Lushan, its delicate flame petals turned back to show dark spots. Ming porcelain of the Thousand Flower pattern, fired in the kilns of Chingtechen, reflect the buttercups, daisies and forget-me-nots we found when we forged ahead of the caravan near the journey's end through secret shortcuts, after we had passed the Lotus Valley road, winding up breathless at the stone cottage high on the ridge, just below the clear cold spring that Mr. Little found. There we could turn and see mountains folding away to the west, the great Yangtze Valley spread out like a map below. I have only to let my eyes rest on my Thousand Flower bowl today to smell the wild grasses, feel the fresh wind let loose from the heavy damp of the flatlands as it swept the meadows, hear my father's seven-note whistle at the far end of the caravan as he kept in touch with us above, my mother's whistle and mine answering his. Once, toward the end of my last golden summer on Lushan in 1934, my friend Frances Smith took me home with her where her father, who was Chiang Kai-shek's pilot, took us for a ride over the mountains. The cluster of our miniature bungalows, the shops and stream winding down through the Gap and the plunge of the Thousand Steps beyond, shrank and were lost in the vast landscape of China.

Although at first my parents occupied different bungalows while senior families were on furlough, in 1925 our family was assigned a double bungalow with the Libby family at the top of Methodist Valley, alongside the stream pouring down from Mr. Little's spring, which was dammed into a pool by our house. This remained our summer home until we left China ten years later, that last summer our half of the bungalow shared with the Haskells, five of them and four of us in the two-bedroom cottage. But there was an enclosed porch Helen Haskell and I made our own, our cots easily lifted out of the way of leaks when the rains came, as they did sometimes for six weeks at a stretch. Libby and Haskell boys bunked in a huge room enclosed beneath the porches set out on stilts from the hillside. There was a cozy, drowsy feel to mornings when we waked, and that was most of them, to the drip of rain in buckets by our beds, sometimes on us, rain sheeting the wall of windows, mushrooms sprouting from the ceiling, and all the crabs from the nearby stream that had taken up residence with us during the night safely gathered into a bucket by my father as he tramped around near-sightedly without his glasses, bathrobe flapping, hair askew.

Helen Haskell and I shared a small chest of drawers with a cupboard on one side in which we stashed rocks and leaves and other treasures, each had our own small red kerosene lamp to light us to bed. As morning brightened and the rains lifted, we would hear the boys stir below, Walter Libby shouting, "Hup, two, three, four" as the twins, Donald and Dorothy, and Alice, my age, marched out with him for exercises and we ran to join them, learning as we stretched and kicked Dr. Libby's song: "I woke up in the morning and looked up on the wall: The cooties and the bedbugs were playing a game of ball. The score was something-or-other to nothing, the bedbugs were ahead. The cooties knocked a home run and knocked me out of bed!" Then we would dive into the pool that never warmed to more than fifty degrees (Mother kept a thermometer immersed in it. She carried one everywhere and could tell you what its readings were by the Dead Sea, in Sumatra or Ceylon, London, Bremen, Paris, wherever we stopped long enough for her to unpack it), and came gasping out for breakfast.

Sunny days we lived in the pool: dragged out the small tin bathtub for a boat, learned new strokes and how to dive from older boys, tangled with water snakes, learned to leave alone the crabs that lurked in rock crevasses at the shallow end when they weren't exploring our house. Mother enjoyed hikes and kept up with the fastest pace set, umbrella in hand for sun or rain, but I never saw her in the pool, while my father, who traveled a great deal by water, thought he should learn to swim. "Jump in, Mr. Hayes! We'll save you!" the Libby boys would shout, and in he'd go with a splash that never got further than a turmoil of flailing arms and splutters. We never noticed when our lips turned blue, but

"They call this fun!" one of the adults shivering in the shallows was heard to mutter.

Someone was always singing in the mountains. "When morning gilds the skies," would come floating up the early morning air from cottages lower on the hillside. "Day is dying in the west," would chorus the whole group gathered Sunday evenings in our living room as we rested our eyes on the long view across to peaks bathed in golden light. There were weeks of gray rains followed by crystal nights when the stars seemed close enough to pick and add to our summer collections of beetles and butterflies, and the aurora borealis flared.

The adults organized swim meets, sings, concerts, amateur theatricals that drew us down the hillsides to the auditorium in the Gap, families converging from several winding paths, lanterns bobbing along like giant fireflies. If it were pouring rain when time to leave for Sunday School, we children splashed down those trails barefooted and in our swim suits and dried off and dressed after we reached the Community Church.

There was no way to go but by foot anywhere on Lushan, and we loved it. There were hikes to the Three Trees, two Japanese cedars and a gingko said to be 1500 years old, watched over by Buddhist monks in a temple set beneath their boughs where there was an old, old statue of Pilou. And who was Pilou? "Look in your own heart," said one of the monks, "and when you come to its deepest place you will find Pilou there." Along the path from the Three Trees that led down to Dragon Pool the characters *t'ing an*, listen quietly, were carved into a rock.

There were hikes to Russian Pool on the edge of a grassy swale where several small streams converged. It was the largest and most popular swimming place, 170 by 30 feet. Sometimes we walked to the low falls and pools known as The Three Graces, my favorite place to swim, where we could dive behind the icy overflow, or shiver, wedged between rocks above the small falls, as the water poured over us. At Emerald Pool, deep and dark and frigid, we never swam and picnicked with care for in early years the unwary had been swept away by sudden torrents. We hiked to Hankow Gorge, Incense Mills, the Cave of The Immortals, each with its special view and meaning, to Lion's Leap where we could see the valley spread out below the sheer cliff after struggling the last hard climb up a steep barren slope; to Nank'ang Pass at full moon with a quick dip in our own pool in the moonlight when we got home, to the Temple in the Clouds, the Three Falls with a drop of 600 feet. For the strong there was the twenty mile hike down the mountain to Copper Pagoda and back.

Lushan meant freedom from restrictions of shoes we had to wear in the valley rife with hookworm, ringworm, impetigo; freedom from clothing as we lived in swim suits playing kick-the-can and statue and prisoner's base; freedom to follow Albert Steward, learning to see Lushan's plants through his eyes, learning to spot the clever funguses we called landstars that could stay for years rolled into dry brown balls, but on being touched with moisture opened into their star shapes. Lushan meant freedom to travel the mountain streams by leaping from rock to rock, sliding slippery ones in a cascade of icy lace. Lushan meant to shiver with delight if we found a fresh tiger or wolf or wildcat spoor, or one dried into mud from an earlier season, for the animals retreated further into the hills as Kuling attracted more and more people. Lushan meant pockets stuffed with rocks and crystals and an occasional fossil shell; toes squishing in wet mud; clear nights lying out under the stars; cicadas sharing our bednets and singing us to sleep; friendships made and renewed. For me Lushan also had space, space enough to withdraw to a vast silence which nourished the inner spaces. Never again, after we left China, would I know such freedom to be plunged into the natural rhythms of life, to be able to drift apart into long stretches of solitude.

But Lushan was not ours. It was only a question of time until the rental period ran out, and each summer more Chinese followed us to the hills. At a Kuling Landrenter's meeting in August 1933, my father made a survey of residents in his usual meticulous fashion. There were 563 houses then built on the lots of the Kuling Estate, with a population of 4,032. Of these, 1,552 were Chinese. Among the others: 974 Americans, 595 British, 189 Germans, 75 Italians, 72 Russians, 49 Swedes, 42 Norwegians, 25 French, 17 Japanese, 11 Finns, and a sprinkling of Spanish, Turkish, Yugoslavian, Danish, Swiss, Estonian, Latvian, Portuguese, Dutch, Polish, Czech and Greek residents.

As I remember Lushan, I am not sure I want to return. From friends who have, I have learned that some of the bungalows, including ours, have disappeared, that there is a military hospital in Methodist Valley and a motor road takes buses and taxis of tourists to what is now a Chinese summer resort. Tourists peer over the cliff at the trail we used; some elect to climb the Thousand Steps as a lark. One friend overheard a tour guide tell his group the resort had been built by "wicked warlords." The Community Church, now a People's Theater, has been the site of Communist Party Central Committee meetings. I have been told that in 1959 the emergency meeting that set in motion events culminating in the Cultural Revolution was held in our church.

Russian Valley was dammed and filled to create Flower Path Lake; the Three Graces pool is now known as Black Dragon Pool and sports a carved rock dragon fountain; two tall stones with a round stone between them represent a pearl, the symbol of purity. In 1985 my sister and daughter could not find the rock below the Three Trees carved once with the characters for "listen quietly."

Are the old rocks still huge against the sky: Cradle Rock and Hat Rock and Pinnacle Rock? Is Slippery Rock, a sheet of water leaving fingers of green flourishing in its cracks, still along the secret shortcut? Is the streambed we climbed to get over the ridge behind our bungalow into the meadow where we could lie for hours on Flat Rock watching the Libby goats, still dry in summer, yielding up its gray, red and ochre clays to probing fingers? Does the old shale path still wind below the ridge? Could I possibly find my way from the main trail along the secret path to the site of our bungalow, or as far as the stone pillars engraved with the number 69 that marked our valley? Does the stream still pour along the Gap, where we climbed rickety stairs behind Mr. Duff's provision store to his ice cream parlor in a lacy wooden *ting-tzu*, pavilion open to the air?

When I ask these questions I find less need to return than to acknowledge that the mountain and river, immense essentials in my world, shaped me as deeply as the people in my life.

Paul G. Hayes

Gatehouse on Ta ma-lu leading into the Ichishan compound. During the 1931 flood Ichishan was an island where the Yangtze had leapt its banks and spread out for a hundred miles. When the Japanese took Wuhu, it was at this gate that Dr. Brown stood off soldiers many times, saving refugee lives.

Lewis L. Gilbert

Community Union Church in The Gap, Kuling, where years later, or so I have been told, those meetings were held that led to the Cultural Revolution.

Heaven Opens,
Earth Shakes

The tramp of feet and shouted commands, followed by a voice raised in anger, drew me to peer out the bathroom window in the Shanghai apartment of friends where we were visiting the summer of 1931. The window overlooked the Kuomintang army drill grounds, where an irate commander walked along each row of men standing at attention, counting them off by tens. At each tenth count the man knelt and was beheaded. So it was I learned the meaning of "to decimate." Several days later I overheard the adults talking with disbelief about a rumor that for some minor infringement of discipline to which no one would confess, an entire Kuomintang company had paid in this manner.

The times were turning uglier for the Chinese, but the only change in our lives that summer was to spend it in the city instead of the mountains. We had gone down to Shanghai in July so that my father could have further medical attention for chest pains that alarmed doctors. We went down river aboard the TSMS (twin screw motor steamer) *Wusueh*, built in Hong Kong, which was on its maiden voyage returning from Ichang. Diesels had been in use for only about ten years, and this was the first Yangtze vessel so equipped, similar to German, Danish and Norwegian cargo ships that passed Ichishan.

While classed as intermediate, with prices we could afford, the *Wusueh* was outfitted first class, and my father explored the whole ship with delight. He shared his cabin and jaunts around the steamer with me; our amah bunked with Mother, while the cook and boy slept on a lower deck. We were all on deck to watch the turn out of the broad expanse of the Yangtze near its mouth into the Whangpoo River, lined on both banks with great industrial plants, while steamers, warships and cargo vessels from scores of nations were anchored along the twelve miles to Shanghai. Then the bund came into view, dominated by the Customs House, the Sassoon House and the Hong Kong & Shanghai Bank.

While he consulted the doctors, my father preached for the vacationing pastor at the Community Church in the French Concession. We lived in its manse and had use of its Hupmobile. My father got French and International Settlement drivers' licenses for which he had to pass stiffer tests than were required in America; in later years in America he loved to produce his Shanghai licenses when stopped for speeding. He delighted in the freedom the car gave us, took amah, cook and boy along on family picnics to Jessfield and Hongkew parks, to Luna Park with its merry-go-round and other rides, and to the movies. Mother reveled in the opportunity to Christmas shop and to buy a pram for the baby she expected in November. City people, my parents loved cosmopolitan Shanghai, while I mourned the loss of Lushan and my dog Pete for a whole summer.

With more leisure that summer of 1931, my father brought his journal up-to-date, noting that ten mission universities previously staffed entirely by foreigners were now headed by Chinese. Then he took time to answer a questionnaire from The Laymen's Inquiry. The mission boards, faced with dwindling income after 1929, had been cutting work budgets: the field projects which included salaries of Chinese pastors and other workers and maintenance of schools and hospitals. When they started to bring missionaries back to America, the laymen, whose gifts made mission work possible, suddenly realized the magnitude of the crisis and decided to see what they could do to save foreign missions.

They organized themselves into the Laymen's Inquiry, with an office in New York from which they addressed questionnaires to thousands of missionaries in major fields around the world, in all major denominations, followed by Approval Committees who traveled to the countries to get firsthand information.

Cheered by the breadth of the questionnaire, my father was unaware that gathering forces would override all thoughtful plans for reorganization. In China, the Nationalists were in grim pursuit of the Communists, who had been driven into the countryside and had elected Mao Tse-tung chairman of the first All China Soviet Government. Chiang Kai-shek led two annihilation campaigns against the Kiangsi Soviets without success, the Reds melting into the peasantry so that it was impossible to tell who was and who was not a Communist, and villagers were slaughtered. The Nationalists continued in pursuit, so intent on their effort to rid China of Communists that they gave no heed to reports from the peasants that the Three of the Midlands (the Yangtze, the Yellow River and the Grand Canal), shamefully neglected by both Ch'ing dynasty officials and the Kuomintang, were rising. Dikes had not been built nor kept in repair for more than twenty years, canals had not been dredged. It was common talk in the marketplace that at the next season of rain the Three would sweep over their banks causing such devastation as had not been seen for centuries. Loaded with what possessions they could carry, those who could left their homes as a ceaseless downpour of rain marked the month of August, followed by typhoon.

Shanghai, although low-lying, was not flooded, the delta there wide and close to the sea, until the typhoon uprooted trees, blew down fences and flimsy homes and sent Whangpoo waters through downtown streets, stores and basements. Flood and typhoon came just as my father was assembling twenty-six pieces of luggage, the pram, three servants, wife and child and thirty-eight parcels of linens and mattresses for Wuhu Hospital sent to the steamer in his care, to return upriver. But the steamer never came, and twice he turned in tickets for steamers that never arrived. Finally he loaded us all aboard a very small boat that took three days to reach Wuhu, edging its way down the Whangpoo that had spread over the delta, past great Empress and President liners that looked like warehouses afloat on the fields, then feeling its way upstream where the river channel was all but lost in a vast expanse of water.

Wuhu was unrecognizable.

Gongs had tolled across the city, summoning the people to sandbag threatened dikes, but on 24 August, swollen waters rushed down from the mountains to the West to overcome the Yangtze, breaking dikes and flooding city streets along its length, drowning light plants, destroying crops, bringing all businesses to a standstill. Usually a mile wide at Wuhu, the river averaged twenty miles in width between Hankow and

Shanghai and at Wuhu left Ichishan an island in an expanse of water more than a hundred miles across, its main channel fifty feet deeper than usual.

As the last Wuhu dike broke under the onslaught of typhoon, yellow water engulfed the city, more than 12,000 people were stranded on hills and high ground, another 40,000 on hills in the nearby countryside, while untold numbers perished. Wuhu Hospital staff, gathered on the roof of the hospital, watched as chunks of the dikes loosened by the torrential rains were picked up and tossed into the air by the wind. People ran screaming in every direction as fields and homes quickly submerged, scrambling to straw roofs only to have mud walls collapse beneath them.

We reached Ichishan by sampan from the steamer, where we found that water had come through the walls at two places but that its high ground was safe and already covered with people crouched in makeshift shelters. Trees were drowning where they stood, mold grew as we watched. Surviving chickens and pigs were gathered on a small raft that served as a market. I saw an old man spread-eagled across the bottom of an upturned tub slowly turning in circles in an eddy below our wall, no one able to respond to his cries, until a current caught and swept him out of sight beyond the *ichi*, which was but another swirl, its craggy outline under water. Pete worked herself into frenzies trying to protect us from the refugees, and we could not convince her that we weren't in danger. As I dreamed up wild schemes to escape into the countryside with my dog (where she certainly would have ended up a meal for the hungry), my father took her to Hyla Doc to be chloroformed.

Colonel Charles and Anne Lindbergh, on their flight *North to the Orient*, offered their services to the Chinese government to survey flood damage and stayed at Ichishan to do so. We watched the small hydroplane circle our hill as they puzzled out where to land and brought it down safely on a flooded field where they sat quietly reading as they waited to be found. The Lindberghs won everyone with his reserve and her warmth, their impressive intelligence coupled with a commitment to be of service. My sister, born that November, was named for Anne Lindbergh, with whom I shared birthdays. Although I was only eight and sat on Lindbergh's lap listening to the adult conversation, both made so deep an impression on me that I followed them closely through the press and their writings down the years.

Wuhu and the flat lands for miles around were under water for one hundred and ten days. Then came winter and famine. Knowing that in flood and famine more people died of disease than of starvation, everyone geared up for the cholera and typhoid to follow. The hospital staff, headed by Dr. K.B. Liu, organized into the Neighborhood Mercy Society, contributed money from their own pockets for rice, clothing and medical care and gave up much of their own food to the refugees while serving the hospital and clinics throughout the emergency without pay. Those of us who sat down to meals in our own homes would look up to find hungry faces pressed against our windows and shared our food too.

The Chinese government appointed its Minister of Health as Director of the Department of Hygiene and Sanitation in the National Relief Commission. They requested Wuhu Hospital to organize sanitation and health work in the Wuhu area and to open an emergency hospital and clinic. Branch clinics were also opened in Chaohsien, Hochow and Ningkuofu, and fifty police students were trained to inspect and direct sanitation in refugee camps. To overcome the refugees' fears of cholera and typhoid inoculations, these students marched through the camps sporting armbands and waving flags that promoted the shots with slogans, helped the medical teams set up borrowed benches or tables, then rolled up their sleeves and asked for shots. In a few short weeks more than a thousand refugees had been inoculated, and within the year the number in Wuhu alone reached 99,000. We took our turns in the lines, all our servants going with us to get their shots at my father's expense.

Refugees, paid in flour sent from America, were employed to keep the camps clean, to sprinkle chloride of lime in the latrines and other fly-breeding places, and to repair roads and dikes as waters receded. Soup kitchens were organized, but these proved hazardous, as it was not uncommon for some of the weak and elderly and the very young to be trampled to death. I remember one old man, trampled and thought to be dead, who was carried to a little mat shelter by the roadside which was all he and his wife had saved of their household. His wife bargained away the shelter and her cooking pots for a coffin, only to see his leg move and discover he was alive. One of the hospital staff reached him just as he was recovering his senses only to discover everything he and his wife had owned was gone. Lying back in his coffin he said, "It is warm here. I will wait the end." He was taken to the hospital, but three days later suddenly died.

Schools were organized for children too young to work but too old to stay with their mothers all day, and for five months were given two meals each day and taught characters, games and lessons in citizenship. While all these emergency measures were being taken, the normal work of the hospital continued, for Wuhu was an endemic area for schistosomiasis, and tuberculosis took no holiday. Patients arriving with Japonicum invariably arrived too late to be saved, beriberi was common. Later in the year Hyla Doc reported increasing numbers of farmers brought in with gunshot wounds or burned in torture by bandits who robbed them of their meager supplies. Flood and famine always swelled the ranks of bandits, China's most visible form of unemployment.

In October my father reported to *The Shanghai Evening Post and Gazette* that the flood in our area had receded about two feet from its high of thirty-one feet, six inches, and that some roads were appearing. The Nanking Government Official Flood survey, based on those made by the Lindberghs and by the University of Nanking School of Agricultural Economics, found that the Central China area had suffered more damages than average, with the Wuhu area hardest hit. Eight and a half million acres of farmland had been flooded, an estimated fifty thousand people drowned and millions more were left homeless.

Chinese and foreigners alike were assessing property damages, and our mission suddenly realized its deeds were in disarray, with many missing. My father was appointed to unearth, systematize and translate the three by four foot documents, a job that took him to Shanghai on numerous trips over the next three years and resulted in an indexed book with English translations and negatives of 187 deeds. He was now fluent in Chinese, preaching without an interpreter, but he needed help with the texts of the deeds and Pastor Liu often accompanied him.

In November 1931, more chest pains plaguing my father puzzled doctors who had ruled out tuberculosis, heart trouble, an infected tooth and swollen tonsils. They cautioned him not to overdo, but that month he was again appointed secretary of the Annual Conference and editor of its official minutes. He was also elected both secretary of the mission and treasurer of the powerful Central China Finance Committee.

It was difficult to find missionaries with business training to fill these positions, and my father had known for some time that his name was coming up in connection with both jobs. He knew more administrative work would further postpone the teaching he hoped to do, and he knew his good friend, Robert Brown, had a record of conflict with every treasurer he had worked with. So it was with a heavy heart he wrote Mother from the 1931 Conference that he had been elected to both posts. Should he accept? Friends counseled that the work needed his systematizing ability, that they believed a way was slowly opening for the seminary teaching he wanted to do and that meantime he should wait patiently and do what came to hand.

Reluctantly he accepted the files, account books and funds in Shanghai banks, the responsibility to represent missionaries and Board in New York to each other according to official actions, handling all correspondence for budgets, furloughs, programs and problems. As treasurer he came into immediate and repeated conflict with his peppery, strong-willed and impatient friend Robert Brown, and placed his resignation in the hands of his bishop. But it was not accepted.

There were three additions to our household that November: a fine new paint job on the house covering up the worst signs of deterioration, Bishop Birney's upright piano which gave us much pleasure before it disappeared into the maelstrom not long after, and my sister, Lois Anne. She grew quickly into a sturdy, golden-curled, blue-eyed charmer, a joyous child with an off-beat sense of humor that endears her to us to this day.

Anticipating that he would be directed to make further cuts in local work, my father took a swing around his country stations early winter 1931 to see how they had fared. He found enormous flood damage to churches and parsonages, the water still six feet deep in some fields. At the January 1932 Finance Committee meeting in Shanghai, faced with cuts up to thirty percent, he was thankful to learn that Bishop Birney, who was dying of tuberculosis and had suffered a stroke, had made a personal gift of $3,000 to the Mission. This made possible a continuation of the most essential work and workers. For the new bishop, Herbert Welch, who relied heavily on him, my father searched for other sources of support. Income from some property rents and an increase in some Chinese contributions were all he could muster.

While in Shanghai, my father wrote Mother that Chiang Kai-shek, who had again resigned as Commander-in-Chief during conflicts with the Canton-based leaders and had left Nanking, seemed about to return. The Canton-based leaders had tried to form a new government, but man after man had resigned while those who remained seemed unable to handle renewed outbreaks of banditry and the Japanese threats from the north. Quick to take advantage of chaos following the flood, the Japanese had invaded Manchuria, the start of fourteen years of undeclared war. My father was sure Chiang would return, on his own terms and with a stronger hand, and that with all his faults Chiang had given China the best government since the revolution began.

On the steamer returning to Wuhu he ran into an old friend, Francis Kales, who was agitated over the action of the Japanese in Manchuria and was leaving his Japanese wife, with whom he lived in the Chinese city in Shanghai, in order to protect her from charges of subversion because of her American husband. "Japan believes her hour of destiny has come," said Kales, vehemently adding that Japan intended to take over the whole of China and anyone believing otherwise was a fool.

Home on 24 January 1932 after three weeks in Shanghai, my father was stunned to learn five days later (by rumor, gunboat radio and local Chinese papers) that the Japanese were bombing the Chinese city in Shanghai, violating international agreements by using Hongkew (the Japanese section of Shanghai) and Paoshan (part of the International Settlement patrolled by Japanese police, who aided in the attack) as a base from which to attack Chapei.

Chinese troops threw up barricades of sandbags and barbed wire, but had no defense against bombs, which demolished the North Railway Station, the "Commercial Press too," mourned my father, "the finest printing establishment in the Far East," which published seventy-five percent of the textbooks used in China's schools.

Also destroyed were the Oriental Library that housed a million volumes, including some of the rarest in China, and vast areas of private property. But they failed to dislodge the Chinese troops who took to the rooftops and alleys and sniped at advancing Japanese. Street fighting was continuous, clouds of smoke filled the sky, Japanese marines took the huge central Post Office, disrupting mail service all over China, set up a machine gun in front of its enormous doors and swept North Szechuan Road with continuous fire.

After bombardment and fighting in Shanghai had continued a week,

Wuhu was still peaceful. Mr. Shibasaki, the Japanese consul, and Mr. Sudo, Commissioner of Customs, were advised to leave Wuhu in a hurried meeting of Chinese civil and military officials, who immediately set guards around Japanese property to prevent looting. The Japanese vice-consul, seriously ill and left behind in our hospital, grew worse as rumors from Shanghai worsened. His doctor, K.B. Liu, recognized that he feared for his life and assured him the hospital and its staff were Christian and would give him the same care they would any Chinese. Months later, after a Japanese gunboat had removed the vice-consul by stretcher, Dr. Liu received a letter from him saying the doctor had so demonstrated the real meaning of Christianity that the vice-consul had become a Christian.

Some mail service resumed, and newspapers reaching Wuhu reported the convergence on Shanghai of the largest fighting forces, naval and military, American, French and British, ever brought together in China at one time.

What happened next was an astonishment to those who had contemptuously referred to the Chinese army as the "largest sitting army in the world." Although bombardment by heavy artillery and infantry charges had by then continued for two weeks, the Chinese prevented the Japanese from proceeding inland, then with the help of the US Thirty-first regiment of marines from the Philippines, British, French and Italian troops defended the International Settlement.

By 14 February, the Japanese still calling their action a skirmish, The *Post* reported more than a million people had been driven from their homes, entire city blocks bombed and burned out, thousands killed. One of the saddest aspects was that all the resources of the Chinese government were being poured into the war so that there was no money for flood relief. Food distribution and reconstruction had come nearly to a halt; funds were not even available to unload American wheat shipments waiting at the docks.

In the cold weather the Chinese lived under desperate conditions. Believing all foreigners to be doctors with access to jobs and unlimited supplies of food, they mobbed anyone brave enough to venture out on the streets, and my father would retreat with a futile sense of heartlessness at not being able to help. Walking down Ta ma-lu with Frank Gale, who had come to Wuhu to head up the Anhwei Famine Relief Committee still trying to distribute supplies, he came on the body of a child half-eaten by dogs. Frank Gale vomited and my father returned home to write to friends, "America in depression—mark my words—is still a heaven on earth as compared with China in a year of flood, famine, banditry and war."

In March 1932 my father took a swing around the southern part of his district to determine where further work cuts could be made. He stayed in the unheated mud huts of his pastors, and while heavily dressed retreated to bed early in the evenings to warm up. Flood waters had receded, there had been no bandits for some time, and the war in Shanghai was thought of as far off, except that an army from Szechuan, marching overland to Shanghai, impressed men and boys from villages along the way to move their equipment.

Wheat, barley and mustard were greening, farmers were cultivating mulberry orchards and preparing low-lying fields for planting as he set out. Most of his territory lay within the Yangtze flood basin, where he could see high water marks eight feet above the fields, three feet above the roads. In the hills and mountains beyond, Japanese miners worked iron and coal.

He took the bus the first eighteen miles to Taipingfu, along the first and for some time the only motor road in the province. All other roads were narrow, a foot or two wide along dikes for foot traffic, three to five feet to accommodate chairs, rickshaws and carts. These narrow roads wound in and out along the borders of fields, mounted up on the dikes, twisted for miles along streams and rivers, then plunged through mud hut villages where dogs barked at his heels and children stared at the foreign devil with his big nose and strange skin.

From Taipingfu he walked eight miles against a stiff wind to Tsaishi to preach the Sunday service, conduct communion, baptize two adults and six children and receive four men into preparatory membership.

Walking on to Changshatu, he visited a church of twenty families who met in a mud and straw-roofed hut like the homes they lived in, then next morning took a sedan chair the seventeen miles to Siaotanyang to visit a church thirty years old. Another eight miles on foot brought him to Powan where the church was in rented rooms, its members tailors, barbers and stone-cutters, a property-less group.

Returning home he walked most of the way to Taipingfu, where he missed the Wuhu bus because it left before its scheduled time. It took forty minutes to find a rickshaw puller willing to face the eighteen miles, and they started out after four in the afternoon, my father with bedding roll between his knees, suitcase across his lap. But the puller, after starting out well, soon showed signs of weariness and admitted he had already pulled for thirteen miles and had had no supper. They walked the rest of the way together by starlight, exchanging pleasantries with other travelers, thankful not to hear rifle shots which in this area had often signified bandits.

Rice, ducks, chickens and pigs were raised for food in this district, straw for the annual refurbishing of roofs, grass roots and tree branches harvested for fuel. There was usually a surplus to sell or exchange for seed, clothing and implements, but the economic margin was close. My father could see no local resources to be tapped to keep the work going as mission funds dried up.

One of the most promising communities in my father's district was Ningkuofu, an important market for rice, dates, bamboo, lumber and charcoal. A city of 40,000 about fifty miles south of Wuhu on the way to Hangchow, in 1930 it had been on the line of march of a rebel army but escaped fire and pillage by a narrow margin. Its only Christian institutions were those of the China Inland Mission and the Methodists who had a flourishing church and a high school, the Wannan Academy.

With a student body of well over a hundred, the academy was the only Christian high school in a large rural area, but differed from the two Chinese high schools only by adding Christian courses to the government-prescribed curriculum, a YMCA and worship opportunities for those who desired them. The thirteen teachers were graduates of the University of Nanking, and its graduates were becoming principals of Chinese schools or serving in the new government. Cooperating with Chiang's efforts to revitalize the country, my father was encouraging the academy to become a training center for rural leadership as well.

As a trustee of the school he was asked to speak to graduating classes and used this opportunity to challenge young men soon to become leaders of new China to take pride in their country's long history and culture and to understand its current problems. He urged them to think independently and to share with their compatriots, who hadn't their opportunities for learning, what they understood to be happening in China. He urged them to learn how complex the issues were, and assured them there were thousands of Westerners eager to help China shake off foreign domination. He reminded them that knowledge is power, and urged them to use that power for the sake of their country, not to enrich themselves.

While my father traveled the countryside, the Japanese landed more troops near Shanghai, then promised to withdraw them if the Chinese would first draw back. The Chinese stepped back twelve miles, but were closely followed by the Japanese, who increased their troops to 60,000 and the Chinese to twice that number. League of Nations investigators arrived and the Japanese made a bid for world approval by withdrawing a few troops. A letter from a Japanese appeared in the *Post* warning Americans not to interfere in Japanese national aims, especially not to boycott her goods, or "the flag of the Rising Sun will soon be proudly flying from the top of the Empire State Building."

There was a build-up of disheartening events. The *Post* reported the kidnapping of the Lindbergh baby. Hundreds of bags of flour that had finally reached Wuhu for refugee relief were stolen. Cholera broke out. Hyla Doc was in bed for several months with suspected tuberculosis. As Mother walked home along Ta ma-lu a Chinese woman tottered up to her on bound feet and spat in her face, while voices in the background shouted "*Sa! Sa!*" "Kill! Kill!" As a group of Chinese pastors returned to Wuhu from meetings in Nanking they were robbed of all they carried with them. The Board of Foreign Missions reported January and February income short another $50,000; that by September missionaries should expect their salaries to be cut another 25 percent, work budgets by 50 percent. My father was advised to sell what mission property he could. Ceilings in our house, soaked with the high humidity, fell down.

My father spent the long hours at his desk necessary to keep four sets of mission accounts and to expedite the heavy correspondence that relayed between New York and China the increasingly disastrous news. "I suppose I have been tamed down considerably," he acknowledged, "for I find myself willing to take over this monotonous work, even though I know it will make it almost impossible for me to do any further writing and research. But it's a matter of necessity. I must do my work as assigned in the mission or face the possibility of joining the ranks of the unemployed. This is no time to quibble about the kind of work one must do."

At the September 1932 Finance and Mission meetings in Nanking, Chinese outnumbered the missionaries and continually interpreted bad news from New York in terms of discrimination, their excitement raised to shouting pitch as project after project was dropped or left without adequate funding. By January 1933 the Board telegraphed that further cuts were needed, and by March there was enough money to send the missionaries half their expected salaries. The Board urged them to find other work in China to supplement what they had, reminded them that they were better off in China with a small income and a Mission home than in America without either employment or a house. My father agreed. He no longer looked forward to his furlough, due in 1934, uneasy over the Board's habit of dropping families already in America, and was relieved when the Board postponed it until 1935.

Friends in Michigan chose a strange gift for the hospital just then, a revolving red neon cross for its roof that became a beacon for ships for miles up and down the river. The Japanese war continued; all Wuhu crossroads were sandbagged. In June a typhoon took the roof off Hyla Doc's house, the chimney crashing down to narrowly miss Grandma Watters.

My rollicking sister proved a delightful distraction to the times. She found the wastebasket a source of great interest, practiced winking at anyone she could get to stand still, wore her little red hat at a rakish angle, even to dinner and to bed. She sported a little red toothbrush with which she solemnly brushed her few teeth, joined family prayers with a "men" at the end, and carried a little wooden stool everywhere with her, setting it down with great ceremony and backing up to sit down on it, often missing it altogether. She would sit contentedly at the doorway watching the puffy little launches on the river. She thought it nice to wear one shoe brown, one black, one high, one low. She was well and strong, and liked to try to stand on her head. Not shy, but busy and talkative, she went easily to everyone to practice her favorite words, "medcin" and "vaccin-ation."

A blessed summer on Lushan brought welcome relief from heat but not from responsibilities. There were only ten families in our valley that summer of 1934; the other fifteen bungalows were rented out. My father continued to serve on the Sanitarium Committee, and with the deaths of two of our number was swamped with burial and estate work. Nor was

132

he relieved of the conflict between liberals and Fundamentalists, who divided into "Love God" and "Fear God" groups on Sundays. One of the Fundamentalists continually identified him with modernism in theology associated with the *Protocols of the Learned Elders of Zion*, an insidious book many Fundamentalists were taking seriously. According to the *Protocols*, the Jews, through a secret conspiracy, were achieving a world empire by taking over the world gold supply, press and education, using sexual perversions, economic crisis, world war and revolution to achieve their goals. It was a relief for my father to put argument about this dangerous nonsense at a distance as he listened to warnings that Reds were headed down river and might surround Lushan. We returned earlier than usual to the heat of the plains, where he received instructions from the Board to "shorten the line" even more as a further loss of $100–200,000 in income for the next year was expected.

The broad background to the Thirties was made up of three major forces beyond the famine and pestilence following on flood and typhoon. Chiang Kai-shek tried to unite and revitalize China and free her from foreign domination. The conflicts between Nationalists and Communists moved into high gear, while the Japanese seized what opportunities opened through domestic chaos to push her bid to take over China.

It was hardly obvious that the domestic conflicts would leave the Communists as China's dominant force, and my father followed General Chiang's career closely. He believed Chiang to be a realist who understood that his armies would only drive the Communists into more and more inaccessible places, and applauded Chiang's efforts to go to the root of the matter with economic programs better than those of the Reds. At Chiang's invitation various Christian missions, including ours, assumed responsibility for the economic and spiritual reconstruction of severely damaged parts of Kiangsi Province, while the government set in motion the New Life Movement. Chiang's program for the rejuvenation of China, the New Life Movement was modeled on YMCA methods and publicly based on the ancient Chinese virtues of propriety, righteousness, integrity and the sense of shame. Unknown to the Chinese people or to the missionaries who backed the movement, behind it stood Chiang's secret Blue Shirt organization patterned on European Fascism and devoted to militarizing the nation under Chiang's control.

My father could see only that Chiang was working against tremendous odds, without the full support of provincial governors and their troops, and saw no one else on the stage of public affairs who gave any hope of doing as well. The decade following 1927 included the most creative years under Chiang's leadership. Roads and railroads were built and extended, programs in rural reconstruction and mass literacy were launched, hospitals and schools built, the currency unified, opium brought under control, and China was well on the way to freedom from domination by the West. A strong, united China was a threat to Japanese goals, the Japanese invasion a tribute to the achievements of Chiang's programs.

By the fall of 1932, the Chinese Communist Party had successfully checked Chiang's first four extermination campaigns against them by using guerrilla tactics that drew the Kuomintang forces into the mountains. Late in 1933 and into 1934, Chiang changed his strategy to follow a systematic blockade of the Communists while invading their area along a line of blockhouses. With encirclement a real possibility, more than one hundred thousand Communists broke out of their Kiangsi retreat by night, and in the legendary Long March, fighting continuously, some of them reached Yenan on foot a year later.

During 1933, as the conflict between Chiang and the Communists intensified and the Japanese were on the march into Jehol Province in the northeast, our area was free of major calamities and unusually free of banditry as more normal life resumed. Wuhu Hospital had four clinics in regular operation and devised insurance plans for the school of the Christian Church mission and for staff and employees of the first railroad under construction in Anhwei. Dr. K.B. Liu reported two cases of eclampsia that year in addition to the usual diseases, the discovery of chronic lead poisoning, and noted that more early cases of tuberculosis came for hospital care. Two battles yet to be won were to make blood transfusions and autopsies acceptable to a people shocked by them.

I remember *The Shanghai Evening Post and Gazette* for its comic strip, "Tillie the Toiler," which featured the muddle-headed antics of a secretary, and was only vaguely aware that my father was a *Post* correspondent. For this he received his subscription, the only way he could afford it. He reported on modernization programs of the new government in extending railways and highways and street widening as these touched our province, and was especially interested in the improved transportation to

Ningkuofu. In early years it took two days in small boats to travel the fifty miles, but by June 1932 he was able to go halfway by bus and the rest by train. Five railroad bridges built in 1907 by the American Bridge Company had stood unfinished and unused for more than twenty years. The new government finished four of them, but the one halfway between Wuhu and Ningkuofu, with no planking over its last 300 feet, had had no power vehicle of any kind pass over it, not even a wheelbarrow, although coolies crossed its girders on foot. By 1935 it, too, was completed, and my father made the trip in three hours.

By 1934 eight airfields were projected for Anhwei, and several interprovincial motor roads. The Wuhu city wall was being demolished and replaced with a highway, while other streets were widened and straightened. A year later most places in the city could be reached by bus, traffic police became a new and prominent addition, and the hospital Ford was no longer the only car in town. Modernization even brought a soap advertising man to Wuhu who ran a bus sporting colorful ads on its sides and made himself welcome by showing "talkies" in the hospital chapel—a Mickey Mouse reel, another on Peking, one about birds and a thriller about airplanes.

The Wuhu Department of Public Works secured a tract of land of over 100 acres, including the highest elevation in the city, for a public park with trees, shrubs and walks giving access to a well-preserved pagoda. During the Lunar New Year these roads and the park were filled with excited crowds creating a flourishing business for restaurants, hotels and photographers. Paper lanterns included modern ones shaped like airplanes, and while the dragon dances still drew crowds, by 1934 they hardly competed with a ride on the railway, open for a few miles, a ride I took along with hundreds of bemused Chinese, all of us intoxicated by the blur of passing fields into a mossy carpet from our great speed, possibly fifteen miles an hour, along an unsettled roadbed.

By April 1935, there was outstanding improvement in transportation, the highway to Nanking kept in good repair with better busses making regular schedules. A new bridge made the time-consuming ferry ride over the Tantu a thing of the past, and reduced travel time for the sixty miles to Nanking to about three hours.

The road was hazardous, however, with pigs, donkeys, carts and pedestrians wandering across without looking, and accidents were numerous. My father and I returned to Wuhu from Nanking on a bus that backed us into the river we had just crossed by raft, when the driver accidentally shifted into reverse; later he slewed off the road within sight of the Wuhu depot in an effort to avoid some pigs. The bus came to a rest sideways against a slender line of willows ringing a pond, and we tiptoed out the back door to complete the trip on foot.

Another time I was with Hyla Doc in the hospital car when we knocked down a farmer herding pigs. We wrapped his bleeding head in bandages for my injured leg, which had occasioned the trip, then spent hours in the Nanking police station as driver, Hyla Doc and farmer each shouted his version of the accident.

Then there was the hot day my father started out all in white from topi to shoes, carrying the small black suitcase that went everywhere with him, and returned many hours later brown from head to foot except for the sides of his suit, which were black.

After the bus had gone some miles down the road it started to rain. My father sat near the rear door, but like everyone else was at the mercy of rivulets turning to brown streams of water that sloshed around the bundles of vegetables and baskets of geese and ducks tied to the top of the bus and poured through cracks in its ceiling. The road soon churned into deep mud and the bus came to a halt. The driver disappeared into a teahouse, for help, my father thought. After a while a man at the front of the bus decided to see what kept the driver, climbed over everyone's feet to reach the door, then silently returned the same way, his feet heavy with mud. After this had happened several times, my father looked at his own feet, decided there was no longer any reason not to step out into the mess and followed suit. In the teahouse the driver sat casually sipping tea. He had given up. So my father started on foot to return to Wuhu. Soon the paper handle to his suitcase broke, and he hefted the bag, first under one arm and then under the other, unaware the dye was working off onto his suit.

Japanese aggression touched us only tangentially. Feelings against the Japanese peaked in Wuhu one night in 1934 when a flotilla of destroyers patrolled the Yangtze in a show of strength and reached our city after dark where they anchored with searchlights playing up and down the bund, probing into the homes of Chinese and foreigners alike with their message of take heed and do as we say or we can destroy you. Hsiao

Bao, Hsiao Shih and I watched the destroyers round the bend coming down river as we stood with the families from the huts among the willows, the babies unusually silent as they sensed the mood. Soon after, the Episcopal school was commandeered by government troops for military training.

Another day, we on Ichishan looked out toward the river to discover guns of the Japanese gunboat trained on us. A hurried call to the Japanese consul sent him to inquire the meaning of the threat. A shot had landed on the deck of the gunboat, which was believed to have come from our hill. Mr. Shibasaki knew this couldn't be true and convinced the nervous navy that it must have been a stray shot from a duck hunter across the river.

The domestic conflict touched us more directly. We had been getting snatches of information about Chiang's campaigns against the Reds, and some missionaries were being caught in the paths of the armies. In May 1934, Howard Smith had been captured by the Communist Fifth Route Army in Penhui, Szechuan, where he and Gertrude worked with villagers on the banks of the Wu River in the Christian Missionary Alliance mission. Gertrude and two-year-old Ray were sent down the Yangtze in a small boat to deliver a $3,000 ransom note, and came to live in our home while Gertrude, whose brother and a cousin had been killed by the Communists, awaited the birth of Anne. Howard was marched off into the mountains with 5,000 troops under General Ho Lung. Because it was understood that neither the US government nor the mission boards would ransom captives, after fifty days' march and watching his chances, Howard escaped one night when his young guard dozed off. Within moments the alarm was sounded, and searchers passed within touching distance several times without spotting him. He continued to evade capture as he snatched grain from the fields and begged raw eggs from farmers while he walked what he later estimated to have been about 800 miles in all before he reached Wuhu.

Then late one afternoon in December 1934, when the ochre light of a cloudless, windless winter sky melted with that of the burnt umber river running in a quiet expanse only hinting at the turbulence of treacherous currents beneath, Hsiao Bao, Hsiao Shih and I left the field behind the great dike flung up against the river to return to the compound.

There was always something astir at the gate, but that day our curios-

137

ity was caught by more than usual agitation. A woman half-turned and shouted at me to stay away while others stepped back from where they had gathered around two open coffins, not an unusual sight, as prudent patients often brought along their own. Without premonition I pushed past the distressed woman to see for myself what absorbed the crowd, and recognized my friends John and Betty Stam, their severed heads wrapped in place with rags.

So it was that the turmoil of China struck at my own life. Among the many missionaries who came and went or stayed a time at Ichishan, John and Betty had become my special friends while they waited for their first child to be born. They were but twenty-six and twenty-seven, and had been gone from Wuhu only a few weeks after Helen Priscilla's birth as they started their first assignment with the China Inland Mission in Tsingteh, about a hundred miles south of Wuhu. It was John, tall and rangy, balanced astride his bike who teased me one day after I absent-mindedly drank Yangtze River water straight from the kitchen spigot soon after returning from Lushan where a spring flowed to our bunga-low. Chang Shi-fu, shocked, told me what I had done. Then Hyla Doc, to whom I confessed, thoroughly dosed me with potassium permanganate and I turned generally purple. Betty, her round white face set off by thick black hair drawn to a generous bun, could always be counted on to yield to my begging to read me her poems. One about birches, a tree I had never seen, still holds magic for me from her gift of words.

The Stams were in the path of a Communist army of 6,000 that reached Tsingteh on the heels of rumors they were in the vicinity, and quickly took over a district where people, already facing famine, saw what was left of their meager supplies disappear. When the army aban-doned the village next morning, they left dead villagers behind and car-ried away captives, among them John carrying Helen Priscilla and Betty on horseback, who smiled at the few people they passed on the familiar road to Miaosheo, twelve miles away. It was years after I stumbled on their bodies at our gate before I learned Betty had been raped. It was weeks before I learned that their captors had discussed in front of them whether or not to kill the baby to save trouble, and that this would have been done but for the unexpected protest from an old farmer.

"Then it's your life for hers!" was the retort.

And he gave it.

Helen Priscilla was left to cry alone in an empty house.

Later identified as the Red-Northern-Campaign Anti-Japanese Army, which had been driven from its headquarters in Kiangsi by Chiang, their commander called the villagers together to witness the punishment of foreigners who represented a government that was helping Chiang to destroy them.

The town was silent for two days after the beheading, and no one dared go near the abandoned house where the baby cried. But slowly those who had fled to hide in the mountains, without shelter or food, began to trickle back. Among them were Pastor and Mrs. Lo who had arrived in Miaosheo the day the Reds reached the village, and had not been identified as Christians. They were worried about their own son who had become ill from exposure. When they heard the whispered story about John and Betty, they gathered up the bodies to be carried in litters, placed their son in one basket hung from a carrying pole and Helen Priscilla in the other, then walked to Wuhu, hiding by day and paying for food with the ten dollars Betty had pinned within her baby's garments. Hyla Doc found Helen Priscilla to be unharmed. Her parents were buried in our cemetery, near our dear Dr. Hart.

Throughout China, missionaries stunned by the proliferation of such incidents tried to learn what they could about these Communists. They searched out specialists knowledgeable about China's agrarian problems, Communism among students, Communism in Russia, child welfare in Russia, rural cooperatives. Aware that in America those disenchanted with an economic system that had fallen into the Great Depression looked with interest toward Marxism, they wondered in what ways Communism might be considered an ally to Christianity in the efforts to solve China's problems.

During this time following the crash of the American stock markets, when a quarter of the work force of the powerful United States was unemployed and thousands wandered her roads looking for shelter, food and jobs; when the missionaries in China did not know whether each pay check might be their last, nor when their turn might come to be caught between opposing Chinese armies, their spirit was "perplexed but not dismayed," as my father summed it up in his report to *The Shanghai Evening Post and Gazette* of how John and Betty had died.

The Lindbergs on the steps of Wuhu General hospital with Frances Culley, Helen Hayes, Gladys Harmon, Dr. Hyla Watters, her mother Ida S. Watters and Dr. Robert Brown. My sister Lois Anne, likes to say she is in the picture, too, for she was born soon after the Lindberg visit and named for Anne Lindberg.

Paul G. Hayes

Col. Charles and Anne Lindberg on their flight told in Anne Lindberg's book, *North to the Orient*. They came down in a paddy field at Wuhu, where Dr. Brown, standing on a pontoon below Col. Lindberg, found them and arranged for their transfer to Ichishan. They gave the Chinese government valuable service surveying the flood.

My sister Lois Anne, in 1934 with her kindergarten friends at the Episcopal Sisters' compound. She was a cheering spirit in a world that was growing increasingly ominous.

Paul G. Hayes

Howard A. Smith

Ray Smith and my sister on Dottie Brown's old rocking horse, Black Beauty, 1934

A Dubious Honor

WHEN A CART HAS PASSED,
IT IS KNOWN BY THE MARK
IT HAS LEFT IN PASSING.

— CHINESE SAYING

Calling American laymen fault finders, in a "devastating document that repudiated most of the efforts of a century," some missionaries discredited one of the few history making documents of contemporary Christianity. *Re-Thinking Missions*, written by The Commission of Appraisal headed by William Ernest Hocking, was published in 1932 by Harper & Brothers.

Frank Rawlinson, editor of *The Chinese Recorder*, asked my father to clarify the report's aims, methods and implications. He threw himself into that effort. He believed it proposed a vigorous, wide-ranging and practical plan. It called for a single organization with administration vested in a central interdenominational committee organized along functional lines to direct evangelism, education, medicine, rural life projects, social welfare and finance. Secretaries would be selected for their experience and ability in each field. Denominational boards would be retained within each church as promotional agencies.

Stirred by the imaginative thinking of the laymen, my father led a study of the report by missionaries on Lushan, then back in Wuhu on his own impulse prepared a study of the practical possibilities of such Protestant cooperation, and soon learned how complicated the mission scene had become.

He focused first on Anhwei Province, which is not a clear physical unit divided at its center by the Yangtze, as a quick look at the map might suggest. Its northern half is largely part of the Hwai River flood plain, its southern part mountainous, dominated by Huangshan. Its 1935 population was estimated at twenty millions, about that of New York and Pennsylvania combined, in about sixty percent their size. Four areas of Christian work were administered from outside the province, due to difficulties of reaching them from within the Anhwei borders. He eliminated them from his study.

About ninety-three percent of the 73,388 Christians in the rest of Anhwei were Catholics, administered from three different Jesuit areas, while the 5,000 Protestants were in twelve missions in overlapping territories, with control centers in half a dozen Yangtze ports. Each of these twelve was responsible to a separate supporting board in the United States, each maintained its churches in harmony with its own doctrines. Less than half were linked to several unifying efforts already underway.

The Methodists themselves were among the most divided groups in China, eight bodies reported in 1922, which had been united into five divisions by 1933. But my father's study found that the members of these five arms of his church lived in fourteen provinces, were widely scattered without modern transportation, and were separated by dialect as well as by geography. Other denominations were at work in those same areas.

As he realized it was work together or perish, and that a slow movement was already underway in this direction, at least within the denominations, he prepared a memorial for the East Asia Conference of 1934 urging that a Commission on Church Unity be authorized to study unions already made and the practical possibilities for others. Such a commission was formed, with Bishop Welch as chairman and my father as secretary. There was a real disposition on the part of the missionaries to solve the problems involved.

The study, prepared by my father at the bishop's request, was his last opportunity to take an active part in making real his vision "of the magnificent Christian impact which a united Church could make on the life of China." He already knew his work would be interrupted by furlough in 1935, but he also knew Bishop Welch and the Central China Conference expected his return.

On 4 January 1935, my father received a letter from the Correspond-ing Secretary of the Methodist Board of Foreign Missions in New York expressing "very great and sincere regret that it is necessary for you to surrender the work in the field to which you have given yourself with earnestness and ability."

Faced with diminishing funds, the Board had "scrutinized its lists of those due for furlough, and had in mind the question of the ability of those who return home to fit themselves in places in this country, and have agreed that we must count on you as one of those whom we will ask to sacrifice."

Having carried the responsibility to implement the Board's direc-tions to cut spending as his major task in recent years, my father took this letter at face value, writing in response that he and Mother felt it a double honor to be selected "to sacrifice for the general good" and to have been chosen on the basis of their "supposed ability to fit into the job field in the United States." Because their income would cease on 30 September, he informed the Board he had written friends among pastors, professors and bishops in America asking for help in finding employment.

Two months later the Board expressed appreciation for his "beautiful spirit," and counseled him to abandon his travel plans through Palestine and Europe because the Gold allowance for his return travel would be cut by $100.

When news of his dismissal became known, letters poured into our home from all over China. Both resident bishops wrote they had no prior knowledge of the Board's decision and had asked that it be reversed. Fel-low Methodists penned many letters of indignation, then recognizing what the Board's move meant in terms of income, they voted unani-mously that the Hayes salary to the end of 1935 be charged to their Mis-sionary Reserve Fund, and that money saved through salary cuts they had taken the year before be granted the Hayes family for 1936.

Friends from many other missions echoed the lament of W.C. Mills of the Nanking YMCA, "We can ill spare you," and of Oswald Goulter of the Christian Mission, "If you leave China, the cause of truly enlightened Christianity suffers a loss that is serious indeed." But first among them all was Frank Rawlinson, whose own American Board had withdrawn eighteen missionaries the previous year. "Why is it that so often these withdrawals have to do with people who are progressive like yourself? I am very sorry *you* were selected for this dubious honor."

He answered his friends, "It is surprising what peace fills our hearts. We just believe that the Lord will make all these things work together for good because we are among those who love Him. Your prayers and good wishes are part of the undergirding of our hearts these days."

In response to the furor created by his dismissal, my father's future was held in a state of uncertainty for the next eighteen months, the Board keeping his name on its lists while he found a new job, but never implementing his posting. Meantime he and Mother packed for furlough and he planned our trip.

He would receive $1,040.90 for our passage, figured by the direct route across the Pacific. He would receive en route, if we went by way of Palestine and Europe as he had planned for so long, his salaries for the months of June, July and August, a total of $1,503.40. He could do it.

When on 25 May 1935 we boarded the *Tuckwo* in a rain so heavy that Ichishan was all but lost to view, my father had $332 Gold and a fistful of tickets in his pocket as we started the three-month journey to the land where Jesus had lived, to Europe and New York.

The *"Tuckwo"* and Other Endings

THE WORLD IS FULL OF MEETINGS
AND PARTINGS, JOY AND SORROW,
LIKE A PERFORMANCE ON A STAGE.

— CHINESE SAYING

When the Yangtze steamer *Tuckwo* pulled away from the Butterfield & Swire hulk in a downpour of rain in May 1935, I stood at the rail straining to see Ichishan.

My parents still believed they would return to China, but that they would leave me in school in America. Standing in a crate on deck, to hold my possessions when I would be left behind, was a chest that had been fashioned from a camphor tree. Its boards had been planed and stacked behind the Libby's stove in Nanchang to dry out over the winter, then carved by men in the local jail with dragons around its sides, gardens, teahouses and camelback bridges on its heavy cover that fastened with a brass lock.

The painted eyes of majestic junks, colorful flags dripping from the masts of half a dozen freighters, the ensigns of British and Japanese gunboats, and two indistinct figures standing on the dike by the huts among the willows, all faded into the blanketing rain. Suddenly I knew there would never be an amah to do for me again. I went down to my cabin and washed out socks.

Between 1935 and 1937 Japanese aggression in China increased. After July 1937 Japan invaded China in force. We had been gone for more

146

than a year when World War Two began for us 14 August 1937 on the north shore of Lake Superior where we had driven for my father's vacation. He was once more a pastor, in Minneapolis. While Mother spread our picnic supper on a rock overlooking the lake, a western sun slanting gold across its waves while Norway spruce soughed between us and Canada, my father turned on the car radio for the evening news.

Before Frank Rawlinson's Shanghai friends learned what had happened, we knew by short-wave that he had been killed by Chinese bombers aiming for the Japanese flagship *Idzumo* tied up at the Nishen Kisen Kaisha pontoons in the Whangpoo in front of the Japanese consulate.

Over the next several years we got disjointed news of what was happening in China, from returning missionaries who stayed in our home and through press and radio reports.

In November 1937, Wuhu was softened up by repeated Japanese bombings on the outskirts of the city and the airfield, built after we left, four miles from Ichishan. The US Ambassador and consuls had urged all Americans to leave the war zone lest there be incidents that would involve the United States. But as they watched the bombings from the hospital that shook with each blast, Robert Brown and Brownie, Hyla Doc, Loren and Ruth Morgan (both doctors who had come to Wuhu during our time), Frances Culley and Florence Sayles (who had come from Chinkiang after our hospital there had been merged with the Wuhu hospital after 1927), made the decision to stay that ninety percent of the missionaries made. They knew the Chinese Red Cross and Chinese medical practitioners in the city would have to leave, that there would be no one but themselves to help the sick and wounded.

As the bombings increased the last three days before the city was taken 10 December 1937, a solid mass of crowding, pushing, frightened people poured along Ta ma-lu (which had been widened into a highway past the hospital gate) as they made for the open fields and grave-dotted hillsides beyond. The Ichishan gates were opened and they were invited in, although no one could promise them protection.

Then the *Tuckwo* was bombed. Jammed with refugees, it failed to get away from its mooring before taking two direct hits that turned it into an inferno as winds blew it back against the hulk, passengers screaming and jumping from its flaming decks. The old hospital Ford sprang into life, protected only by a small American flag flying from its bonnet, as it went forth with Robert Brown at its wheel to gather up the wounded, who filled the hospital wards and overflowed into corridors and chapel.

Chinese and Americans heaved sighs of relief when they saw Japanese soldiers marching into a city already deserted by the Chinese military on its move westward, expecting a well-controlled, disciplined army to reestablish law and order. But the next morning they saw Japanese soldiers hunt down civilians much as they might rabbits, and Robert Brown went to the commander to ask protection for Ichishan, which was promised.

Our once-thriving city of 200,000 was reduced to two to three thousand persons as killings continued and those who were able fled westward on the great trek then underway. Not only individuals scrambled for safety, but a mass migration of China's armies, factories, businesses, universities and hospitals picked up what could be carried and moved on foot, by boat and bus, a distance comparable to moving from New York to Omaha or Denver.

During that winter and spring of 1938, not one of the 3,000 people who trusted their lives to Wuhu Hospital was harmed, although for some weeks Japanese soldiers continued to climb over the wall demanding loot and women, and had to be escorted out of the compound. Every shop and residence in the city was looted, and shiploads of materials left the Wuhu bund for Japan. Many times squads of soldiers arrived at the Ichishan gate and demanded women, circling Robert Brown with leveled bayonets. On one occasion he stood them off for an hour and a half, insisting the Japanese government had promised the American government not to interfere with the work of American institutions, that if his hospital (famous throughout America, he told them, hoping he didn't stretch the truth too far) were forcibly invaded, the news would be all over America within twenty-four hours. The officer in charge finally sent his men off and accepted Dr. Brown's invitation to tea.

Robert Brown reported each incident to the US Consul General in Shanghai, who relayed the news to Washington. A year later, while in Japan to restore his confidence in the good Japanese he knew were there, he was drawn aside at a party by Ambassador Grew who showed him a fat Wuhu file and congratulated him on the way he had held firm. The Wuhu Japanese had received instructions from Tokyo to leave the hospital alone because they were causing too much unpleasant publicity.

Local Japanese harassment then began to take subtler forms (blocking supplies from Shanghai, refusing travel permits or permission to give inoculations or vaccinations) until the work of the hospital was brought almost to a standstill. The culminating episode revolved around men from a French gunboat who had been invited to use the hospital swimming pool and supplied with one pass for the entire group. Sentries at the gate insisted each sailor had to have his own pass and refused them entrance. Hyla Doc, unwilling to give up while Robert Brown was away, set up card tables and supplied the sailors with games of pick-up-sticks until Dr. Brown arrived and insisted that since the area outside the gate was hospital property and the sentries had already admitted them, that they should go on in and have a swim.

The missionaries were amused by the whole episode, but the Japanese chose to take it as an insult to the Emperor, and Dr. Brown's value at the hospital was greatly diminished. Realizing that increasing troubles were due largely to his combative presence, he accepted the invitation of the National Christian Council and the Chinese Medical Association to coordinate the work of the 268 mission hospitals in China with that of the Chinese Red Cross, the army medial service, the International Red Cross and American-British Relief. For distinguished service, particularly his later efforts to diminish malaria along the Burma Road, Robert Brown was decorated by Chiang Kai-shek.

Meantime, Dr. Loren Morgan and Dr. Ruth Morgan, Hyla Doc, Frances Culley, Florence Sayles and Paul and Stella Sommerfreund, Jewish doctors who had escaped Hitler, kept the hospital going until Pearl Harbor. Unknown to them, young Chinese doctors and orderlies put to use the Morse Code Hyla Doc had taught them, sending to Hankow by radio advance warnings of Japanese movements. The Chinese knew none of the missionaries could successfully dissemble, should they learn the truth and be questioned, and kept their radio secret, frequently changing its hiding place. Mystified, Hyla Doc entertained wave after wave of Japanese officers searching for it. One, whom Hyla Doc found to be particularly unpleasant, poked into every corner, then on the hospital roof leaned against the balustrade to light a cigarette and question her further. Shocked to believe it of herself, Hyla Doc suddenly wanted to push him overboard. The Japanese never found the radio, and it wasn't until 1980 that Hyla Doc learned its true story when some of her former students, now surgeons at her old hospital, told her about it.

Hyla Doc got letters out of China without Japanese censorship by way of navy friends who passed them on to marines in Shanghai, who in turn smuggled them out of the country. In this roundabout way we learned something of what was happening, as well as Hyla Doc's excited report that one clear night as she walked home from the hospital she looked up and there, where she and Grandma Watters had always said it must be, was the Southern Cross. When we had looked for it before, it had always been obscured by cloud or by dust from the Gobi. But Grandma Watters was not to learn the good news as she had died while visiting another daughter in India.

By 1938 Wuhu was no longer on the front lines but a base of supply for the Japanese push into the interior. Troop movements were continuous, ranks of hot and weary men on the march dressed in heavy khaki uniforms not suited to the Yangtze Valley summer, while reconditioned tankers and freighters, sometimes twenty-seven or thirty at a time, unloaded artillery and cavalry on the bund.

The Japanese did everything they could to bring the work of the hospital to a halt. They threw obstacles in the way of buying enough rice to feed the Ichishan community, enough coal to keep up minimum steam, enough drugs to treat the sick. But rice was spliced out with wheat obtained in part locally and in part through the Red Cross. For fuel for cooking and boiling water the hospital turned to wood, cutting first the diseased trees on Ichishan, then buying wood cut in the country and brought down the small streams by sampan to Wuhu. Laundry done without benefit of steam-run machinery was far more laborious, but could be done. In the operating room Hyla Doc went off the "steam standard" and revived the earlier practice of running a small sterilizer over charcoal and having boiled water poured over her hands as she scrubbed.

"Well, the game being played," wrote Hyla Doc, "is an attempt to make us lose patience and get fed up, and quit. And just for that we won't. . . . Meantime. . . we've been having more than two hundred in-patients in our 150-bed hospital. That's more than ever before, barring cholera and nearby battles. This is neither, just the usual run of sick people. Some we put on the floor, and some we send home days before they ought to go, and some we push out much against their will, but still they come. I've got to comb the men's surgical ward tomorrow morning to eliminate those who can possibly go home, for the crew are staggering on their feet."

Illness had also cut the ranks of the staff, and Wuhu doctors often relied on the help of American ship doctors in port. Hyla Doc was especially glad when the *Oahu* arrived, for Dr. Creeman was "keen on surgery, and good at it. . . . Two of the non-medical officers [were also] keen on surgery, and we've 'scrubbed them in' on operations too. The Executive Officer helped me amputate a leg two days ago. At the critical moment I handed him the saw, so it was really he who took off the leg. Of course if it came to war [between America and Japan] it might be a valuable thing for several of them to have had some experience of that sort. This same man has been repairing all our radios, thus putting us in touch with the world."

On 8 December 1941, which was 7 December in the US, seventeen missionaries attending Annual Conference on Ichishan were gathered around Hyla Doc's breakfast table when they looked up to find a Japanese sentry with rifle and fixed bayonet in the doorway. "Thou preparest a table before me in the presence of mine enemies," murmured Hyla Doc, as they learned of Pearl Harbor.

Dr. Loren Morgan was taken from the table by the Japanese, but was allowed to attend Sister Constance, too ill to be moved to an internment camp. Bishop Ralph Ward was taken from the breakfast table and interned throughout the war, first in Shanghai then in Shantung, suffering hunger, privation and torture. Hyla Doc reached Shanghai with the first group and was for some months allowed to treat Chinese, Russian, British and American children, then adults as well. Hopping on a bike to travel between the women and children confined in one camp and the men in another across the Putong River, she became adept at passing messages back and forth without moving her lips as she gave examinations, injections or transfusions. Soon she was confined with the others, and was in the last group of repatriates, nearly two years later, to be loaded onto the *Tia Maru*, a French passenger ship commandeered by the Japanese early in the war. They were shipped off to Portuguese Goa where the repatriates were transferred to the Swedish *Gripsholm*, and reached New York 9 December 1943 by way of Port Elizabeth, South Africa, and Rio de Janeiro.

In 1945, determined to return to Wuhu as war ended to repossess the hospital if she could, Hyla Doc traveled under US Army orders across India, then flew into Free China. In Chengtu she served in the new hospital built during the war on the West China University campus to train medical students, while she waited to take a sampan down river to Chungking. It took five days to reach Chungking. Her nervous boatmen, who were really farmers, flew an American flag to discourage bandits. They landed at the American Air Force Base, and when it looked as though they would arrive stern first, Hyla Doc couldn't bear such a nautical disgrace, grabbed the sculling oar and turned the boat around.

On the first steamer to make the down river run in 1945, Hyla Doc joined Loren Morgan who had made his way upriver after being released from internment in Shanghai. Back on Ichishan they became sandwiched between the Japanese army, which had retreated to the hospital at the top of the hill, and the Chinese army at its base. Both armies, fortunately, considered themselves to be protectors of the foreigners.

When the tense hours were over and surrender negotiations completed, Loren Morgan and Hyla Doc surveyed the filth and desolation that had been Wuhu General Hospital, then hunted up the red neon cross the Spanish Sisters had successfully hidden, and led a triumphant procession back to the wrecked building.

When the Japanese had turned it into an army hospital in 1941, they walled-in the five big sun porches to provide Japanese toilets, and stench pervaded the whole building. The children's ward partition had been knocked out and the ward combined with a hallway to provide baths. Some equipment had been saved by the Spanish Sisters, but most had been stolen or destroyed. The grounds and road had been dug up for fortifications and air raid shelters.

Surgical, laboratory and ward equipment had disappeared. The steam engine and boilers, water system, generators, pumps, motors and auxiliary machines had ceased to function. Screens were missing, doors gone, and all the windows had been smashed. Chinese planes had got a direct hit on a Japanese freighter loading ore downstream from the hospital (headed for Japan to be turned into ammunition) and the concussion had knocked out the big plate glass operating room windows, huge windows that could never be replaced as the cost was too high.

The Japanese had uncoupled all the radiators and thrown them out of the windows. Then they tossed out surgical instruments and medical books. But the horrified Japanese army doctor collected what he could, cleaned off the mud, stood the books in the sun to dry then replaced them on their shelves. He hunted the hillside for surgical instruments, cleaned and sandpapered off the rust, put broken parts together, vaselined the lot and put them into a zinc-lined chest in the operating room and piled things on top. When he turned the room back to Hyla Doc he told her what he had done. He had studied medicine in America and was much worried as to what his old friends, reading about atrocities in their papers, would think of him. "I told him," said Hyla Doc, "his old friends, knowing him, would think better of the Japanese people in general. He was a very fine person."

Loren Morgan and Hyla Doc recommended that a competent Chinese who was not a physician be named to tackle the job of repair, rebuilding and re-equipping Wuhu Hospital. Luckily for everyone, Colonel Gilbert Nee approached Bishop Ward at about this time to ask for work. Originally from Foochow, Gilbert Nee had studied in the United States and returned to China in 1941 as a liaison officer in the Chinese army. His last assignment was to supervise the disarming of 20,000 Japanese soldiers near Shanghai. Uneasy with army assignments, unwilling to go into government service, he placed his gifts of leadership and business administration at the service of the Methodists. Under his guidance and with gifts from the International Red Cross, the American Red Cross, the British and Canadian Red Cross, and a grant from Chinese National Relief and Rehabilitation Administration (CNRRA), Wuhu General Hospital once again came to life.

Loren Morgan and Hyla Doc were assigned temporary rooms for an outpatient clinic inside the gate and were assisted by four nurses who served without pay. A temporary kitchen was put into operation, and the 300 smashed windows that let in rain, wind and thieves were replaced. Slowly the building was cleaned and repaired, and on 1 April 1946 the main hospital and the second and third floors of the west wing were reopened. On 18 April the Nursing School reopened with thirty-six students and fifteen graduate students. On 25 May the first floor of the west wing began to function.

Irene Shih was named Superintendent of Nurses, Frances Culley, back from the Philippines, the General Nursing Supervisor. In tribute to Culley, Colonel Nee wrote, "She is the one much credited with building up our nurses' training school to the highest in the nation. She was for years superintendent of nurses herself, but she purposefully stepped aside to give place for developing Christian Chinese leadership. To this pioneer woman I pay my tribute."

All over China returning missionaries followed suit, placing in Chinese hands the reins of leadership. When it became apparent in 1949 that China missions would come to an end, when the last missionaries left in 1951, they knew their work remained in capable hands.

Courtesy Carrel Morgan

From Ichishan a stunned hospital staff watched Japanese planes bomb the *Tuckwo,* 5 December 1937.

Courtesy Carrel Morgan

Wuhu General Hospital in 1937 with the second wing added to the right, built of the bricks and on the spot where we children had built a playhouse.

Elsie H. Landstrom

Wuhu General Hospital in 1980, now the teaching hospital for Wannan Medical College. The Red Star has supplanted Hyla Watters' porthole.

The Mountains
and Rivers Remain

THE NATION MAY TOPPLE, BUT
THE MOUNTAINS AND RIVERS REMAIN.

— TU FU (712-770)

Lt's not too bad. They just whip you," drawled Vinney as he sauntered back to the lounge in Shanghai where in the summer of 1980 our Columbia University language study group waited. He was the first of us to be called before a panel of teachers for conversation and reading to determine our class placements.

Going to China as a student plunged me into a group of young Americans full of energy and high spirits, already knowledgeable about Chinese history and culture, some with several years' study of the language behind them. Willing to try anything, they coached Chinese students in English, played extras in the filming of a movie, took an impromptu "Ben Hur" race down the main campus thoroughfare when they found two untended three-wheeled carts outside our dorm, saluting the huge statue of Mao as they passed. Some accepted invitations to take part in volleyball and soccer tournaments and in swim meets, while others went out for *t'ai chi*, probably unaware that until about 1900 no missionary efforts or examples could induce Chinese scholars or students to shed their long gowns or risk breaking long fingernails in sports. A classic joke among missionaries was that, seeing four foreigners running, jumping, sweating, pursuing and knocking about a tennis ball, an observer inquired, "Why don't they hire coolies to do that?"

Going to China as a student gave me nearly three months at about the cost of a three-week tour, with a far better chance of reaching Wuhu. The night before I left, Hyla Doc, then eighty-seven, who had lectured at Wuhu Hospital earlier in the year, gave me the name of its director and chief surgeon. She suggested I write to Dr. Li on arrival in Shanghai and ask him to invite me back to Wuhu or I might not get there. This I did, and followed the advice of our Columbia director to apply immediately for a Wuhu travel permit.

I learned of the Columbia-Shanghai program four days before applications were due, barely had time to dread the heat, humidity, crowding, dirt, illness, long hours of study and restrictions that I knew lay ahead, half-hoped to be turned down as I slid my application into the mailbox, before I found myself on Korean Airlines en route to Hong Kong, then walking across the Lo-wu Bridge. I had never seen the bridge before, except in imagination as I followed those who came out of China across it and those who returned, half expected to meet Bao Ruo-wang* in his government-issue suit with one dollar in his pocket who walked out across this bridge to freedom in 1964 after seven years in prison. As I slowly dragged my suitcase across the narrow iron span in disbelief to be actually walking into China, her green fields shone ahead through unexpected tears.

In Canton (Guangzhou) we exchanged train for China Airlines, landed in Shanghai in a downpour of rain and were met by teachers with a school bus. "Why didn't they tell me Shanghai was so dingy!" was my inward wail as we drove to East China Normal University (on the campus of the mission-founded St. John's University) far out in the western

---

* Bao Ruo-wang (Jean Pasqualini), whose father was Corsican and his mother Chinese, was brought up at home as a Chinese boy but educated in a Western Catholic school. He was a French citizen, although he had never been out of China, married a Chinese and in 1945 was an interpreter for American marines in Beijing. His arrest in 1957 by the Communists was inevitable. When France and the People's Republic of China formally recognized each other in 1964, he was released as a "special gesture of extraordinary magnanimity." His harrowing story of seven years as a prisoner, tempered by his wry humor, *Prisoners of Mao*, written with Rudolph Chelminski, is well worth reading by Westerners.

suburbs. Of course I knew the elegant Western metropolis was long gone. Of course I knew there had been no building or maintenance through ten years of Cultural Revolution and much destruction. Of course I knew many large building projects stood half finished, less expensive to abandon than complete. Of course I knew millions had been sunk into Western-style projects that, once completed, lacked personnel skilled in management, operation or maintenance. But while I was prepared for a genuinely Chinese city, somehow my imagination had not conjured up her shabbiness. Later I learned this deterioration had been caused by the central government in Beijing "milking" Shanghai, leaving few funds for its own use. This policy changed and Shanghai has become a great, modern city.

Our building on campus, newly cleaned and repaired, painted and equipped with Western plumbing, new furniture and bedding, shone in contrast. It served as both dorm and classrooms. In the dilapidated dorm next to ours, Chinese students and interpreters for our program (students of English who hoped to polish their skills while helping us) lived eight to a room where we were two.

Two of the young interpreters were named Hsiao Bao and Hsiao Shih. I did not tell them what their names meant to me, but welcomed their company that first day when they walked with me in the park beyond the back gate of the school, speaking that mix of English and Chinese they so fervently hoped to increase to English and we to Chinese. "It is raining cats and dogs," one of them remarked, when we ducked into a pavilion as the daily rains began, "is that good idiom?"

As we settled into our dorm we were overwhelmed by a swampy sewage odor rising from the waterlogged athletic field nearby. Each hot, humid day thereafter, I washed my hair, myself and every stitch of clothing in the water we were warned not to drink. Every day the *ayi* (the word *amah* is no longer used) mopped down all the floors, which never seemed to dry. I ceased to smell the swamp and wondered whether I had taken on its fragrance. Other pollution, raw sewage in the two rivers running through the campus where small boys swam even when they had been warned not to; coal dust settling over papers on my desk, coating the fan blades, drifting over the bed; the clang, day and night, of industries powered by soft coal, gave me a hint of the problems China had yet to solve.

I was sick. Constantly. My plumbing worked not at all or in too great haste. My temperature maintained a steady hundred degrees and I couldn't stop coughing. With a history of allergies, I hesitated going to the infirmary with other students who were plagued with coughs that deepened into bronchitis, then pneumonia for a few of us.

After a black interval during which I believed I had overestimated my strength, would be a drag on the program and should return to the States, I rallied what resources I had to plan my survival, and received a tremendous boost when given a small room to myself.

Somehow I stumbled through those long days of unaccustomed study, mostly memorization at which I am not adept, but did not miss class. Our teacher was clear, precise, good-humored. Without a word of English she brought each lesson alive, then left us in the hands of one of the English-language students to tackle the grammar.

As in my childhood, the tug of the streets was irresistible, and I went out alone as often as I could, stopped to sip the weak version of iced coffee in corner shops and found myself peering, perhaps too closely for Chinese comfort, into Chinese faces. They peered back. Too many of them were coolies. The word "coolie" has rightfully been struck from the language, yet there they were, the young men and women capable of so much more productive work heavily laden with the transport chores of the nation. I wondered what else lived that was denied. They crowded about me by the hundreds. We laughed over my funny Chinese, their funny English. They plucked at my blouse. I told them their shoes and shirts and jackets and blouses, their bobbed hair and perms, their umbrellas, all looked Western to me.

I saw no pockmarked faces. No rags. No beggars. No running sores. No twisted bodies. No dead babies rolled into gutters. I saw young faces. Healthy faces. None of them were alive when I lived in China. Startled, I realized their memories were not my memories, their China not my China. Gone were the three million residents of the Shanghai I once knew; walking her streets were twelve million newcomers.

Each face was strikingly different. Perhaps here was the germ of an answer as to why my parents went to China. Missionaries did not expect to change China as a country but to bring individuals to an experience of Christ. They were caught up in the larger issues through China's own needs. Hudson Taylor in 1886 wrote with an impassioned hand of the "million a month dying in that land—dying without God!" But to most missionaries the Chinese were the one, two or three touched by the story of the carpenter god.

Although the streets were as noisy with voices and the clatter of daily life as I remembered, it was a far more mechanical noise. I missed a good-humored bantering, a spontaneous screaming of invective that would subside into amusement or triumph. In nearly three months I saw only two incidents of bad temper, once when a mother suddenly whacked her child, and again when one of two men arguing at an early morning street market was dumped among the cabbages. There was a feeling of lethargy among people assigned sometimes three or more to one job, to underline the government's claim of full employment.

Stories seeped out about the Cultural Revolution, and we learned that the vice-president of our university was one of those frequently beaten who finally leaped to his death from a window. We heard a murmured "it was a disaster" from time to time, and some of those queried quietly told the tragic tales that have become so familiar, while others disappeared behind traditional Chinese laughter in the face of the unacceptable, their faces turning red, their eyes inward and unseeing.

My eye was constantly caught by the small dwellings that housed in a couple of rooms whole families who in summer (what did they do in winter?) were using the sidewalks to cook, hang out the wash, cut one another's hair, chop up the fowl or clean the vegetables, brush their teeth. These small houses had the distinction of grace in line but were rapidly being torn down to make way for apartment houses, bleak cement blocks that are long-lasting in a climate of damp and termites but hard on weak lungs, aching bones and the spirit.

I was full of questions I hesitated to ask. Would I cause embarrassment or danger? Letters were a part of my own survival plan, but when I sat down to write I found my pen poised in indecision, knowing that international mail was censored. Out on the streets I knew nothing I did went unnoticed. I knew that to be watched and reported on has been a part of Chinese life for centuries, that perhaps the sense of surveillance I had was no more than Chinese curiosity. How well I remember fingernails at oiled-paper windows of Chinese inns scratching holes for the curious to watch the foreigners. But behind the genuine, often kindly, curiosity stood the reality of the street committee or work unit, the *tan-*

wei , through which government intruded into the most private family life. When I mentioned to a Chinese friend that I did not believe I had been followed, he countered, "How would you know?" Students allowed to talk with us would suddenly disappear, or were curtly turned from our dorm door. We didn't know why and our questions went unanswered.

When I reached Hong Kong at the end of the summer I reacted to the sybaritic city with unexpected relief. No one looked over my shoulder. No one expected me to think or act in any particular way. No one else decided the shape of my day. I did not need to hold my tongue for fear of causing harm.

There was no one in all Shanghai for me to search out on my parents' or my own behalf, but new friends materialized whenever I stopped to ask directions in a city that retained a general familiarity. Wedging my way onto public transport was sometimes no less an endeavor than to wedge my Anhwei burr into the general hubbub of Shanghai sibilants, but people passed me along from one to another until someone understood my query.

I found the Community Church, where we lived that 1931 summer of the great flood, by asking the oldest man in a crowd around me after I reached the general area if he remembered a church nearby. It looked much as I remembered it, except for broken stained-glass windows. It was a school for opera singers about to be restored as a church.

At the Moore Memorial Methodist Church, now known as Moan, I found that one of its fourteen pastors remembered my father. Fifteen hundred people attended each of three services at Moan each Sunday; among them some who befriended me and took me home with them.

I visited my college roommate's eighty-year-old aunt, principal since 1932 of what was originally a mission school and is now one of the few "key" of the thousand high schools in Shanghai. Key schools are academically strong, receive extra funds and are better staffed than most. A member of eight municipal and cultural committees, including the Shanghai Governing Council, the principal took me home with her for a delicious meal and told her own stories of five years' confinement to the school cleaning latrines during the Cultural Revolution, cut off completely from family and friends; of how she had not become a member of the Communist Party, but was convinced it was only through its leadership that China could have pulled herself into the self-supporting, self-respecting nation of today.

"What have you seen in China?" this delightful, very sharp old lady asked, and was pleased with my list of the good and not so good. "Tell your friends in America," she said, "tell them the changes you see, both the good and the bad."

One day I went down to the Bank of China on the bund to exchange for *ren min bi* some of the "funny money" issued foreign visitors that was good only in hotels and Friendship Stores. A black market in Chinese currency prompted this funny money, when citizens started lending money to relatives visiting from overseas. They arranged for repayment in equivalent deposits in foreign banks, circumnavigating currency regulations in anticipation of being allowed to travel abroad, and creating a monetary drain the government could not afford.

Granted the *ren min bi* with little question and some attention to the school pin we all wore, I walked out onto the bund where an elderly woman with a basket of wired *tzu tzu-hua* blossoms on her arm looked up and caught my eye. We stood silently a moment, locked in our separate memories of an earlier time, then she reached out and wrapped a wire of flowers around the button of my blouse. I tried to give her the few *fen* for which she was selling the flowers, but without taking her eyes from mine she gently folded my fingers back around the coins, shook her head and walked off down the street.

One of the interpreters stopped by my room most afternoons, when we helped each other with language problems. She had obviously been associating with Americans who had not resisted her entreaties for American idiom, for she solemnly sprinkled through her textbook English such phrases as "Thumbs up!" "Sock it to them!" "Party pooper" and "I've got other fish to fry."

We had tea in her room in the dorm next to ours, her room twin to mine, about eight or nine feet by ten, shared on weekends with her husband who worked in another city. Her scanty wardrobe hung on a string hoisted near the ceiling, and she used a forked stick to lift down garments. Evenings she came over to use one of the two tubs in our bathroom and we would lie soaking and talking.

"A stitch in time saves nine," she commented one day as we climbed into a taxi to reach a tailor she knew to turn my piece of blue silk into an "old fashioned blouse; you should get a modern one like mine," she said, and was surprised to learn that hers looked Western to me.

I seized the opportunity away from the school to let her know some of us were embarrassed by those who did not keep the rules we had all read and signed our willingness to obey. "To err is human, to forgive divine," she remarked, as I went over the list of offenses we had been presented as a group behind closed doors: coming in drunk at three a.m. through the bathroom window, sex in the dorm, tardiness to class, absence from cultural events, cheating on tests, wearing slippers to class. "We know," she went on, "that not all Americans are bad," and nodded thoughtfully. "A still tongue keeps a wise head."

About three weeks after our arrival I managed to down a breakfast of one cold, slippery fried egg chased all over the flat plate with my chopsticks, soggy potato chips, pickles and congee. It went down better than the cold eel of the day before, and I realized I was on the mend. Eel and eggs: I knew I should be grateful for such delicacies, but it was difficult when I saw teachers go by with only bowls of congee.

Something was mended in me beyond my errant digestion and too-high fever. I had felt myself growing short-tempered by the way we were shoved around, by shouting voices, confusion and procrastination surrounding decisions. Life in this way, I began to realize, was much the same as it had been for missionaries, for whom China was known to be a hard assignment of few rewards, many frustrations; the shoving and shouting and agreeableness without action far more difficult to deal with than physical hardships. It had been the common experience to start out, as I had, with high hopes, warm feelings, only to become ill, disenchanted as we were skillfully and smilingly turned from what we wanted to do. And it was common experience to move beyond the miseries. Lifelong love affairs with China are the rule, not the exception.

I was not the only one to have used the language program as a way to reach China for my own purposes. I was candid about my intent, assured it would be possible to return to Wuhu, and told to apply early. I was scrupulous in my class attendance, assignment preparation and at turning up at cultural events, not merely to gain Brownie points, but because I had made the commitment.

One day I would be told I could go to Wuhu, the next that I could not. Four students who wanted to accompany me were definitely turned down. One of my Chinese friends asked, "Maybe there is concern for your safety?" I hadn't thought of that. No one mentioned the three huge locks on our dorm door, nor the wash stolen from our lines.

Was I a problem for whom no one wanted responsibility? Each day I approached someone with my question, trying to work up the chain of command so far as I could figure it out, probably irritating everyone with my persistence. Was indecision merely a concern for me and how well I could manage on my own? Was it a hangover of deference to superiors so that only one at the top could decide? Perhaps there had to be a consensus of our *tan-wei?* Perhaps no one had the time to think about my agenda at all. There was just enough hesitation in the negative answers to keep me asking.

Each time I asked I was asked in return, "Have you relatives in Wuhu?" Overseas Chinese were moving freely about the country; would it have been an easier decision if I had? When I repeated that I was not Chinese, they repeated, "Maybe your mother—?" This mistake was made time and again, by students in our group, by teachers, by Chinese on the streets, then on the train. I was puzzled, for I do not look or dress like a Chinese, my language facility is very limited. Nor could they tell me why. But I am grateful for the mistake, for it made me look more carefully at what created the person I am.

Priority must have been placed on the many problems created by the clash between Chinese educators who expected students to act obediently and in concert, and American students who took as undisputed right the opportunity to scatter and explore Shanghai. Long before our classes reached the lesson on Shanghai's transport system, most of us had found maps showing bus and trolley routes, how to reach zoo and post office, telephone, Peace Hotel and the Jing Jiang Hotel, and of course the department stores and Friendship Store. To their credit in the inevitable jousting of our first few weeks, our hosts quickly gave up expecting us to line up by twos or to stay in class groups with our teachers for lectures as we visited cultural sites. Pressed in upon by hundreds of the curious, jostled by one another's umbrellas, we wandered off, guidebooks in hand. But rules were suddenly tightened, and when you think of it, this is the way it goes in China. Rules are relaxed and tightened so that no one quite knows where he stands or whether that which is permissible today will be dangerously wrong tomorrow.

Our trip to Wuhsi was seared into my memory by an interview and tour on which seemed to hinge the decision about my return to Wuhu. An invitation had reached me from the Wuhu surgeon, which I had passed on to the teachers. It was with some relief and some trepidation that I watched our Chinese director approach me on the train. She sat down beside me in the rocking coach, attendants lugging kettles of water and teacups to passengers jammed into the hard seat coach all shrieking to one another over the racket of the train. She shouted questions to me, trying to find out whether I understood enough Chinese to make my way alone to Wuhu, whether I had friends or relatives there to look out for me, whether I expected to be in the city or out in the countryside, which she believed to be dangerous. I was unnerved into making every possible grammatical mistake as I tried to answer her, and was relieved when a teacher sitting opposite listened for a time, then leaned across and explained that I understood more Chinese than I could speak.

Later, in Huai-shan Yüan, when our young students dashed off in the heat to climb the highest hill, my vision of a solitary cup of tea under an enormous ginkgo, hundreds of years old, was shattered. I was propelled by the director and a teacher in the wake of a local guide who had given up on our scattered group. His full attention was therefore on me as we wandered through this truly beautiful temple and its grounds, telling me tales associated with it out of antiquity, among them how Huang Ti himself, the legendary Yellow Emperor who is credited with the beginnings of all things Chinese, came down from heaven to drink tea with one of the monks and sat right there on that stone seat where I now sat.

With the help of a crowd of listeners that grew larger and pressed closer each minute, the guide's acting ability and simplified Chinese, and my own determined concentration, I managed to understand the gist of each story and repeat enough of it so that he knew I did. Each time understanding broke through the crowd cheered and applauded, and I remembered, wryly, my childhood ambition to be a tightrope walker.

Finally we sat down by a pool where giant carp swam in golden circles under creamy lotus, and our Chinese director settled silently beside me with a smile and a handful of crumbs for the fish, unfurled her fan with that delicate twist of the wrist I wish I could master, and gave me the fan as well.

Next morning I was told the teachers had met in special session and had decided to get me the police permit to go to Wuhu.

But the decision was not followed by action, and I decided to act on my own, took my passport and letter of invitation, jumped into the 67 trolley and edged up to the driver to ask him directions while two men with a tub of water disputed its destination and as we lurched along much of it slopped on me. When I found what I would have called the *yamen* and walked in as though I knew what I were doing, a very thin policeman, whose belt must have been wrapped around him twice, looked up through steel rimmed glasses, fingered my Shi Da pin, asked me to read some characters, then casually stamped a permit while asking me where I came from and why I wanted to go to Wuhu.

Jubilant, I left ready to buy a ticket, took the long bus and trolley ride to China Travel Service in the Peace Hotel down on the bund only to learn that the person selling tickets to Wuhu had not come to work that day. Her ticket drawer was locked, so *mei yu fa tse* , no way, could anyone else get into her drawer or sell me a ticket. On my second try several days later, the lady was present but could not find the Wuhu tickets, her hands fluttering uncertainly over the drawer in marked contrast to the robust figure she presented otherwise. I gave up and returned, fuming, to the school. Then the realization dawned on me that a little delay and inconvenience were nothing to what most travelers in China over the centuries have faced. There were no bandits or demobilized soldiers roaming the countryside to be avoided, there were no armies on the march, there was no war being fought anywhere in China at that moment. During all the years my family lived in China there had always, somewhere, been a war.

IN THE GREAT HALL OF THE PEOPLE on Tienanmen Square in Peking there is an enormous hand-wrought-iron picture of a wind-bent pine, known as the Welcoming Pine. It was made in Wuhu and represents the province of Anhwei. A duplicate hangs in the hall of the factory in Wuhu where it was made. The real pine once clung to the side of the cliff on Huangshan where the winds of centuries shaped it. It looks much like the pine gripped to the cliff on Lushan that we knew as Lion's Leap, a stunning symbol of grace in endurance, one of the popular Chinese artistic themes.

"Grace in endurance," I thought to myself, turning away from the great picture in the Wuhu factory, remembering the iron pictures on my own walls of the Three Enduring Friends, *Sui Han San Yo*. Originally forged to be the four sides of a lantern, backed with orange silk, that hung on our verandah, the three enduring friends (the pine, the bamboo and the plum, with a panel of chrysanthemums to balance them) are still eloquent, their heavy metal delicate against white walls.

The man who made the famous Wuhu "iron flowers" in the Thirties protected his skill, a secret entrusted to succeeding generations of his family. It would have died with him had a helper not drilled a hole in his workshop ceiling, or so the story goes, and watched the process.

Grace in endurance. Surely this is as exact a symbol of Chinese life as one could find. And there it was, in Wuhu.

It required several trips to downtown Shanghai to get my train ticket, but once China Travel Service decided to let me have it they casually offered me my choice of soft or hard seat, of the services of a travel representative in Wuhu if I wished. Having traveled hard seat to other cities, I realized crowded cars meant interaction with the passengers around me when I knew I would want to go home in private. I chose soft seat. And yes, I would be glad to have a CTS man make taxi arrangements for me in Wuhu.

So I rode alone, gripped throughout the eight-hour train ride by the sense of history that had swept back and forth across the vast rice fields and through the mud hut villages with their ponds where flocks of geese and ducks still feed and nest and produce the down making this region famous.

Our diesel was replaced with a steam engine at Nanking, and we chugged slowly into the back country across bridges that spanned rivers we had crossed by raft half a century ago. I watched for the two stone "lions of Liang" that once stood alone in a field, mysterious evidence, in a sweep of grain, of continuity in a countryside tuned to the slow seasonal rhythms periodically upset by war. Whether I missed them or they were gone, their absence spoke for me of change this time more convulsive than China had known for centuries.

After Nanking we passed signs for a number of small towns and villages before arriving at the stop in Wuhu. My permit was checked and a taxi took me to T'iehshan Fan Dien, the Iron Hill Guest House. From the name I surmised I must be near the old Asiatic Petroleum Company and

Missionary Alliance compounds and T'ieh-Fantzu, the Iron House dispensary, but nothing looked familiar.

Wuhu. Reed Lake. The city with this beautiful name bears little resemblance to the city I remember of narrow, walled streets with pleasant wooded hills on its outskirts, where about 200,000 people went about their business. It is a busy city of 2,000,000 today, with wide streets and motor traffic, new apartment houses where I remember rice and rape and mustard fields.

As I first entered my room in the guest house I pulled open a drawer of the writing desk to locate stationery to write my parents from Wuhu, and a knob came off in my hand, adding to the trail of broken thermoses, towel racks and lamps I had left behind me. But as I looked at the worn furnishings in this new building, recognizing them from foreign homes of the Thirties, looked out the window at the dilapidated but vaguely familiar house across the wall, shaken because I am usually careful of things, suddenly the essential spirit of the Chinese to prevail shown through the shoddiness.

Disoriented, and with feelings not quite under control, I called Dr. Li and asked to delay my visit to Ichishan until next day. An unexpected reluctance to look directly at anything in Wuhu rose up in me, and throughout that day and the next it was as though I had to circle with my back turned toward what mattered most. The part of me that knew I had to make good use of limited hours urged me to get my bearings. To do so I took a taxi to the river and walked along the cement quay that has replaced the mud dike and weeping willows below Ichishan.

With my back to Ichishan, immobilized for the moment, I slowly became aware that I stood near a gangway where men and women moved in a continuous line carrying goods from the hold of a small freighter and glanced curiously at me as they passed. I had returned to the spot where I had last stood in Wuhu to climb the gangplank to the *Tuckwo* and where it must have been tied up in 1937 when the bombs struck.

I knew that behind me Ichishan still jutted out into the Yangtze, from the picture I had seen of it in the March 1978 *China Pictorial*. I knew the hospital was still there, that Hyla Doc's house still stood near the top of the hill, the Brown's further down and ours near the river. I knew that the mud huts among the willows were replaced with a ship-building yard that stretched across the steps the coolies climbed down to fill their buckets with water from the river, across Ta ma-lu, through the wall and across our garden to the foot of our house.

Through the blur of heavily-laden men and women moving back and forth between bund and freighter, I looked out at the river, its silky-smooth brown waves carrying my eyes the mile across to the "green fields beyond the swelling flood," in Grandma Watters' words. It was strangely empty, so empty that my eyes focused in shock, and I looked again: no magnificent junks with great eyes painted on their bows, spreading stately sails to catch the wind; no crowding of freighters flying flags from all over the world; no steamships, no warships. There were no sampans, no busy little launches, no women paddling round wooden tubs out to passenger ships to sell produce or scream for handouts as they waved long poles with bags tied to the ends along the rails. There were no flocks of ducks swimming to market, no log rafts, no dolphins stitching their graceful way upstream. Some activity along the bund was not that of the bustling market-place I remembered; perhaps something to do with the three ferry terminals I learned later had been built, one for people, one for trucks and a third for railroad cars hauled across the river three at a time on barges to connect with an engine going north. But nothing moved across the river just then.

Were the buildings along the bund the old Jardine and Butterfield go-downs? Where was Shihtzushan, the Lion Hill of the Episcopal Mission, Fenghuangshan, Phoenix Hill of Christian Missionary Alliance, the towering red brick building of the Spanish sisters, now a factory? Where would the Salt Gabbelle have been, the British Asiatic Petroleum hill, the Japanese consulate, the Customs Club? In what direction lay Second Street? Seeing faces, hearing voices as I looked about, remembering more than forty foreign families, I heard the taxi driver say that I was the only foreigner that day in Wuhu.

When I finally turned toward Ichishan, trees almost obscured our houses. The hospital looked larger than I remembered because of the wing added in 1936, built from the pile of bricks Dottie and I had turned into a playhouse. It looked smaller, too, dwarfed by a white cement building added in 1972.

I got back in the taxi and we drove along the bund toward Ichishan, but had to make a sharp turn, about where the mud huts in the willows used to be, on a road lined with houses where the buffalo field once was, where Hsiao Bao and Hsiao Shih sailed their kites, the old men aired their pet thrushes and the young men staged their cricket fights. There was the windmill I climbed one day in haste with an angry water buffalo in pursuit, all but lost in a tangle of wires that I suppose have something to do with the shipyard.

When we reached Ta ma-lu, it was to find that the old road no longer leads to the Ichishan gatehouse. We had to turn right, back toward the city, to follow what had been the dike between rice paddies that grew into a fine road sweeping up to the hospital gates and finally into a highway around Ichishan down which people had fled the Japanese in 1937. As a child I sloshed down it in rain boots through deep mud, rode rickshaws snuggled down into a warm dog fur robe, sailed down it in sampans during the flood. There is no longer a *yamen* with fine horses tethered at its gate. There are no fields with honeypots, no noodle factory, no slaughter house. But the cotton mill is still there. We drove down a busy commercial street, horn blaring. Where along Ta ma-lu was it that I saw a heavy Chinese gentleman in a rickshaw and looked closely at him, knowing we were soon to leave Wuhu, and wondered how long memory lasted: would I remember the tilt of his head when I was an old lady?

At Shihtzushan we drove up the broken brickway to the top of the hill where the Episcopal school is still a school. I searched for our foreign cemetery, and poking about in the hope of finding a broken headstone inscribed with Hart or Stam I found instead a cabbage field. Back downhill near the gate I looked at an old gray structure with its top section removed and recognized from the arched windows on its remaining floor our foreign-services church. Inside it was filled with machinery. The dusty, dirty far end was where my father took his turn in the pulpit Sunday afternoons. There he preached the sermon against war that sent some of his fellow missionaries out of the church in protest. It was there he learned to keep his sermons to twenty minutes, for if they went longer he was drowned out by the Japanese cotton mill whistle that sounded each afternoon at four o'clock for a change of shift, and again ten minutes later. Once the whole church dissolved in laughter as we reached these words of our closing hymn just as the whistle blew: "Hark! How the heavenly anthem drowns all music but its own."

Circling back to T'iehshan Fan Dien I walked through small shops and picked up rice bowls to take from one hometown to another. As we passed the gate to the customs compound where I tossed Chang Shi-fu's hat into a pond, all I could see was tall, long-unmowed grass. At the guest house I looked again at the elderly, vaguely familiar, house across the wall and recognized under additions the Haskell's house. To take a picture I walked back down T'iehshan and up Fenghuangshan on the other side of a long wall, found myself passing Aunt Bertha's Hatbox set among sunflowers, and Uncle Joe's cottage, his beloved tennis court a vegetable garden.

Then I went to look for T'ieh Fantzu, the Iron House used as dispensary. Its sheet-iron construction had intensified summer heat and winter cold but had seemed indestructible. Where it had been is a two-story pavilion by Jing Hu, Mirror Lake, the mud puddle beside T'ieh Fantzu enlarged into a lovely willow-circled body of water for boating, with carp swimming lazily beneath lotus blossoms. The stream feeding it, is this the stream that flowed through the gardens of my friends, the Wangs? Magic, it always seemed to me, to pass from the high-walled street through heavily-barred gates into courtyard after courtyard filled with chrysanthemums or roses in season, moongates leading finally to stream, willows, a camel-backed bridge and a pavilion where old Mr. Wang sat dressed in his long gray scholar's robe, black silk vest, little round black skull cap, long white trousers, under the gray robe bound tightly around his ankles above black slippers. He gave me my first "four precious things," ink, inkslab, brush and paper, taught me my first characters. He was my own special friend to whom I had been casually brought by one of the nurses who knew the family.

At the Welcoming Pavilion set beside Jing Hu, I found an art exhibit, the only place in China where I did not draw a crowd, Wuhu residents as intent on looking as I was. After studying meticulous copies of past Chinese triumphs, a few gaudy and more flat representations, several propaganda posters, I grew restive as I moved from painting to scroll to poster, until I found one black and white woodcut of a traditional summer scene of boys with water buffaloes cooling off in a pond, a scene that had in it a sudden burst of spirit. A huge tree loomed out of the water dominating the cut, leaning toward the left bank while shading the river and the two buffaloes submerged to their heads. One slight figure, perched back to viewer on one buffalo, looked toward the opposite bank where in silhouette his friend threw off his shirt. In this gesture, the smallest possible line, the spirit blew free.

I am glad I saw that picture. It may be the most important thing I saw in China as I watched for evidences of unfettered and healthy spirit. I remember Ruskin's remark that great nations write their stories in three books, the book of their words, that of their deeds and the book of their art, but of the three only the book of art is to be trusted.

Back at the guest house I was seated alone for supper at a round table large enough for ten and served with four meat and vegetable dishes, tea and orange slices. The employees who sat at the other tables (I was the only guest) eyed me curiously over their bowls of rice, one vegetable and soup. By my second evening meal they accepted my invitation to join me, but refused to share my over-abundant food and all sat together across from me and asked with curiosity but no sign of animosity, why it was I was in Wuhu.

I went to bed early that first evening, listening to the Voice of America as the cicada chorus faded away in the dark, shaken by the unexpected stop of Ta ma-lu short of Ichishan, comforted by the remembrance of fresh young faces of children as they ran after me calling "Foreigner! Foreigner!" with not one shout of "Foreign Devil!"

Next morning, where the golden mustard fields bloomed behind Ichishan, turning April into one of the wonders of the world, I found a new road lined with apartment houses leading to a new entrance. A new road inside the compound wound uphill past the house where we lived and Hyla Doc with us while the hospital was being built, that became Dr. K.B. Liu's home where Dottie and I threw stones. Other, unfamiliar, buildings displaced the graveyard, brick pile, piggery and goat pens; and where, I wondered, has the duck pond gone?

At the entrance to a new building of the hospital, Dr. Li Jing, flanked by members of his staff, met and escorted me to an upstairs room where a table had been set with flowers, apples, cakes and cocoa in thermoses, its windows wide to the city and river.

Through a window to the west I could see the sweeping approach to the old hospital filled with lines of flapping white sheets and gowns hung out to dry, Hyla Doc's porthole sporting a red star, the bronze plaques to either side of the entrance still in place. "Who is my neighbor?" still reads one in Chinese, and the other, "Not to be ministered unto but to minister." The roof garden was across from me, the red neon cross vanished.

These I noted while we exchanged courtesies, and I learned that Dr. Li had grown up in Shanghai during the years I lived in Wuhu. We spoke of many things, skirting those that might not be judicious, and as we spoke I looked out the window toward T'iehshan where the abbot of the Buddhist temple there so many years ago spoke about the gods of Buddhism and Christianity as gods of mercy and compassion, the hope of the future.

I was able to tell Dr. Li something of the early history of this hospital as we walked past my father's office where four patients were wedged into the small room, stopped in the doorway to the chapel, its colored windows still in place, divided into cubicles that serve as laboratory and dispensary. Familiar rooms and corridors were filled to overflowing with patients, more than 500 where there were now beds for 465. When Dr. Li reached Ichishan in 1972, the hospital was in much the same condition as Hyla Doc and Loren Morgan found it at the end of the Japanese war, a consequence of the Cultural Revolution. It was opened with fifty beds that slowly increased each year, and the medical school was built.

We climbed to the hospital roof, the elevator long out-of-order, looked over the grounds where everywhere there were signs of planting and renewal and a moongate invited ambulatory patients into a small garden with a lotus pond and fountain. The hospital showed her wounds in her general air of weariness, repairs to her facade clearly of second importance to the service she rendered, the state of her equipment symbolized by the x-ray machine built in Hungary in 1950.

As we circled the compound, out the water gate and down along the *ichi,* around the three old mission homes, a part of me kept up an animated succession of stories for the four people who walked with me, while I noted the water gate and our old wash house are now residences, the handholds on the *ichi* placed there by Dr. Hart now broken or missing, the *kui hua,* the cassia tree with its fragrant yellow blossoms by my bedroom window, twice the height I remembered it. Gone were the walnut, banana and fig trees, the heavenly bamboo by the front steps, the entire bamboo grove behind the house, the great gnarled wisteria with its thick rope branches. Gone the camellia hedge, the rose garden, the climbing yellow rose Mother brought from Nanking, the climbing white rose and the yellow rose Uncle Joe planted by Hyla Doc's porch from a slip he cut from the bush by Edgerton Hart's grave. A huge cement building filled our backyard, by it a spigot for water where our filter *kang* of sand and palm fibers had stood.

As we circled our house, old when I was a child, where my childhood was packed away in its attic, I couldn't muster the words to ask to step inside. Four families live there now and I hesitated to invade their privacy without invitation. Perhaps even more powerful a deterrent was a reluctance to look full-face at who we are now and who we had been, my father and mother and I, insights that needed to come slowly. As I chattered along, the windows of the old house gave up nothing of past or present, reflected only the news that it had grown old and tired and in danger of falling down.

Dr. Li wore different hats as director of the hospital and its chief surgeon, as Professor of surgery in the medical college. Within moments after meeting we were talking ideas, Dr. Li's vision for the hospital matching the goal set by his country for the year 2000 kindling him with enthusiasm. A proud and austere man, an administrator with ideas, a teacher, a survivor, above all a surgeon, he was passionately devoted to public service. Unmindful of the deprivations and waste of his own life, his thinking ranged to world problems with which he kept in touch through the Voice of America. The force of his integrity, courage and dedication turned what might have been for me merely a nostalgic return into a dynamic connection with Wuhu Hospital.

When I asked him the question I asked each thoughtful person I met, "What would you like me to say to the American people?" he shot back without hesitation, "Tell them we have been friends, we are friends, we will be friends, and we will work together to create a peaceful world."

My father and myself at the entrance to Methodist Valley, Kuling, on Lushan, 1931.

My sister, Losi Anne Anderson and Ruth, my daughter, at the entrance to Methodist Valley, 1985

Paul G. Hayes

At the left is the large double bungalow where we lived on the mountain. The Libby family lived in the far half. 1934

Lois Anderson

Ruth Landstrom at the site of our bungalow, 1985.

The Hong Kong and Shanghai Bank on the Shanghai bund from the Whang Pu River, 1980. This magnificent building was the second largest bank in the world when it was built in 1923 by Palmer and Turner, a British firm. Until 1966 its entrance was flanked by a pair of bronze lions whose noses were rubbed by passersby for good luck. During the Cultural Revolution they were dumped in the basement of the Shanghai Museum. The Shanghai mayor and his large staff have occupied it, but perhaps with the return of the Hong Kong and Shanghai bank it will revert to its origins.

Elsie H. Landstrom

The Welcoming Pine in Wuhu, 1980, is a duplicate of that representing Anhwei Province in the Great Hall of the People in present-day Beijing. It is made of hand-forged iron.

177

Elsie H. Landstrom

Our home on Ichishan, 1980. The house and *kuei hua* tree both survived Japanese occupation, the Chinese civil war, and the Cultural Revolution.

Formal portrait of our group with hospital, medical school, city and provincial government representatives at Wuhu Ichishan (now spelled Yijishan) Centennial in 1989.

Elsie H. Landstrom

In 1980 I found the hospital pharmacy in what had been the chapel.

Closing the Circle

IT WOULD BE A MISTAKE TO IMAGINE THAT BY ACHIEVING
YOUR AIM YOU WILL BRING MATTERS TO A CLOSE.
REBIRTH IS THE KEY, THE ENDING BUT A NEW BEGIN-
NING, CREATIVE POWER CIRCLING FOREVER AND EVER
INTO ETERNITY.

— ADAPTED FROM THE I CHING
HEXAGRAM 64, WEI CHI

They are nearly all gone now, the China missionaries. All those who shared their memories with me as I wrote this memoir—Bertha Cassidy, Walter Haskell, Lucile Libby, Hyla Watters and both my parents—have died.

How remarkable they all were. I salute them as human beings first, Christians second, with all the problems each of us has in reconciling what we profess with the way we live each day. As a keeper of their memories long enough to understand something of what they did and why, I can now relinquish that role with respect for the part they played in trying to make known a god who will endure. Chinese disillusionment with Mao underscores the inadequacy of human leadership that tries to take to itself the power and the glory that belong elsewhere.

Because my parents' generation had to leave behind in China work they believed to be unfinished, they would be astounded to know of the remarkable resurgence of Christianity today. In 1995 Amity News Service (Amity is a Chinese organization that helps Chinese churches connect with the western churches) surveyed membership of the Chinese

Christian Church, the post-denominational organization of all Protestant churches throughout China.

In 1949, when the Communists came to power, there were an estimated 700,000 Protestants in all of China. Amity reports that there are now between 8,500,000 and 12,635,000. For our province of Anhwei, a hodgepodge of overlapping denominational activity that my father surveyed in 1935 with an eagerness to change, Amity reports there are now 850,000 to 1,200,000 Protestants—more than there were in all of China in 1949.

When I described to my father in 1980 the revival of the churches that I had noted, he was delighted that it was the Chinese church for which he had hoped and worked so many years before. He remembered the well-known story among missionaries of the Chinese man who in his perplexity said, "I understand your Jesus, but Presbyterian, Methodist, Episcopal I do not understand." My father would rejoice at the mysterious workings of God.

Many of the questions with which I set out in writing this book have been answered; those that have not I release into the past that has taken all but one of my Chinese childhood friends. Among these questions is the hardest of all: how can we of the East and West understand each other when someone with my background in both finds it so difficult? I know only that we must keep trying and not fall into the trap of thinking we already do.

In the years since my return to China in 1980 I have watched her teeter along on the knife-edge of progress, tightening authority until rigidity sets in, then relaxing the official grip until confusion takes over, possibly the only way for that unwieldy weight of more than a billion people to move. And China has made astonishing changes, no longer looks or feels as she did in 1980 or in 1989. My job as I see it is to keep tuned to what is happening, keep informed but wary of jumping to conclusions, and to serve as a bridge between my two countries as opportunity arises.

Such an opportunity came in 1982 when I was able to bring Dr. Li Jing from Wuhu Hospital to this country. He returned to China full of vigor and ideas after two months as guest of surgeons at Harvard, Johns Hopkins and East Carolina University medical schools and left in his wake a good many thoughtful persons. Unfortunately, once more good intentions brought sad results. Through a combination of what I can only surmise were jealousy of Dr. Li's good luck to have been invited to the US and resentment of his sometimes imperious manner, he was retired from his various positions. Little of the values he gained from his visit here accrued to Wuhu Hospital.

In 1985 a friend and I planned to take our younger sisters back to the China they barely remembered. I was packed, ready to leave, but had my gallbladder removed instead. So it was that my friend stood in for me and that my sister and daughter went to Wuhu and Lushan without me. It was a disappointment to my sister that I could not be there to reacquaint her with hazy memories.

On Lushan they walked through the Gap, found our old library and church, swam at the Three Graces, walked past the Three Trees where there was no sign of the temple or the gentle abbot who once presided there. My daughter carried with her the snapshot of me and my father standing on the steps leading to our valley. We had learned that an army hospital was now located there, so when Ruth saw a group of Chinese in hospital uniforms approach she showed them the snapshot and asked whether they knew where to find the steps.

"Right there," the Chinese said, pointing to one side, where, indeed, the steps still stood and the great rock beside them. But the pillars had been torn down.

My sister, Lois Anne, and Ruth found where the pool had once been built by our home and had their picture taken on the empty house site. They found Cradle Rock, Emerald Pool and a host of other places that touched our collective memory.

In 1989 my circle came full around with the centennial celebration of the Wuhu Ichishan Hospital. I had told Wuhu surgeons that the hospital would reach one hundred years in October, and with traditional Chinese love of celebration plans got underway that included two hundred representatives from other hospitals and medical schools across the land as well as ten of us who stood in for those who had founded the hospital and seen it through its first half century.

Hyla Doc had asked me to represent her at these celebrations. My sister wanted me to be there to say to her, "there was where you sat on your stool to watch the Yangtze pageant, there you played in your sandbox, there you saw the big black snake and right there is where you went to nursery school with the Chinese children."

The hospital had requested that I gather together some of those whose relatives had been an integral part of the history of the hospital, and to write that history for their library. Troubled with back problems, I had decided to make a quick trip in to Wuhu and to return straight home when the party was over. But one by one those I had contacted asked to travel with me, some who had had little or no experience of China. I found I hadn't the heart to take them straight in and out again, and planned a good tour: Hong Kong to Kueilin, Chengtu, Chungking, five days down the Yangtze through the gorges and on to Wuhu. The others planned to fly home from Beijing, while Margaret Berry, who was my companion in my husband's place, and I got tickets for the Trans-Siberian Railroad to Moscow, then Leningrad, Helsinki and home.

The lower reaches of the Yangtze were a special treat for me. Those flat shores along which I traveled so many times as a child astonished me with their abundance of trees and factories. So it was that toward sunset one day our small steamer put in at Kiukiang on our run down river. I had chosen not to debark at Kiukiang, not to return to Lushan. I was content to see the river a wash of gold in the evening light, edged by green and gold rushes and low lavender hills behind them, while dimly visible but unmistakable the outline of Lushan's peaks was etched against a soft salmon-colored sky.

The centennial celebrations were superb, firecrackers ushering in the ceremonies, the large platform of the auditorium filled with solemn Party members. Speech followed speech at this Plenary Session, including one by Carrel Morgan whose parents, Drs. Loren and Ruth Morgan had served the hospital so well during the Japanese occupation. I had asked that his interpreter be Patrick Hu, rescued as a young boy by Hyla Doc during the 1931 flood. Pat also spoke, spontaneously, and paid eloquent tribute to the work of the foreigners who had changed his life.

The Plenary Session was followed by small group forums. At ours Elizabeth Allen, Hyla Doc's niece, presented to the hospital a check for $13,700 given in memory of Hyla Doc along with a framed photo of her and a copper plaque reading: "A gift of love to the people of Wuhu from friends around the world in memory of Dr. Hyla S. Watters on the occasion of the Centennial of Ichishan Hospital, 1889-1989." I presented the hardcover history of the hospital with copies for each of the centennial committee members.

Following banquets and tours of the city we toured the hospital, now the proud teaching hospital of the leading medical school of Anhwei Province. With new buildings towering everywhere, 700 patients can now be accommodated. There are a thousand medical staff, including some 300 doctors and nursing heads, 21 clinical departments, 19 medical technology departments and 15 teaching-research stations. We saw an impressive array of technical equipment, learned about the hospital's involvement in active research and publishing and in a foreign-aid program in Yemen.

Surely the spirits of all those who worked so hard to bring Wuhu Ichishan Hospital into being and carried her through those tough first sixty years, would have been present and smiling on this fine occasion.

To thank us for our part in the celebration, our hosts had arranged a trip to Huangshan, the great mountain that dominates the southern part of the province. The night before we were to depart for Huangshan was dark, the dark of a soft October night, and I wakened from a dream to the murmur of the Yangtze below my window, as I had so many years before. But the dream was new. I turned chilly, then cold, in the hard narrow bed as I slowly became aware that this was 1989, that yes, I was back on Ichishan listening to the river murmuring in its ancient voice, but that I was now an old lady.

I lay awake until the sky lightened, listening to the sleeping hospital, a cough, a voice then stilled. I got up to check on the laundry washed the night before and hung in the bathroom to dry, then dressed and quietly started to pack.

Margaret wakened, and when she was fully dressed and bustling about at her own packing, I said, "I had a dream last night about Huangshan. Something is going to happen there."

Margaret waited for me to go on.

"I dreamt that you were conventional and died of a heart attack; that I, unable to do the walking and climbing necessary, was carried in a chair—and dropped: impaled on one of those thin slivers of rock that rise all around Huangshan. I didn't die."

After breakfast the hospital car and bus set out with us heading southwest along the river, then south toward the famous mountain. Huangshan is a granite mountain of seventy-two distinct peaks that reach 7,000 feet. It is noted for its fantastically shaped rocks, for ancient pines clinging to its wind-swept rocks, for its seas of clouds swirling around its peaks and for its hot springs. To climb Huangshan is to walk into a living Chinese ink-wash landscape painting. Today a road reaches far up the mountain and a cable car lifts the visitor another couple of thousand feet. Beyond that, chair carriers have reappeared along with entrepreneurship to aid the needy. Huangshan is a favorite vacation spot for Chinese officials and important state guests, just as Lushan has been, and an airfield is planned for its upper slopes.

Huangshan is 143 miles from Wuhu, a seven-hour drive through the countryside my father walked over so many times in the past. I recognized the names of small towns we drove through from tales he once told. This beautiful farming country, the heart of the Han rice bowl, was for me the most memorable part of our entire trip.

It was on spectacular Huangshan that I opened my door to the knock of one of our hosts carrying a slip of paper with my Conway telephone number on it and the letters BEDERLAN. If my son, Peter Landstrom, were trying to reach me, what had happened to my husband, Norman? It took four hours to get a line through to Conway where at four in the morning my children waited. Norman had died of a heart attack.

My group was superbly supportive, and gave up a beautiful side trip to accompany me back to Wuhu. All the doctors with us were concerned for my well-being; one took my hand and said, "Maybe God meant you to be with new friends at this time."

Each time, and there had been several along the way, when I had thought I had to return home, something happened or some person turned up who made it possible for me to continue the trip. And why was it that I had scribbled by our phone, just before leaving Conway, the telephone number of the US Embassy in Beijing, which is manned round the clock? Of course, I had sent the Embassy a list of my group members and our itinerary, since the Tienanmen events were not long past.

We waited overnight to go down the mountain in daylight, the start of the five-day return to Conway. Then came the ride, for me by chair while others walked, to the cablecar, the drive down the narrow mountain road with its hairpin turns and a strange noise at each turn that had our driver hopping out to tighten the wheels. Then the seven-hour drive back to Wuhu, hurtling along at perhaps twenty miles an hour on collision course with every goose, water buffalo, truck, cart, wheelbarrow and farmer with carrying pole. In China auto travel is accompanied by continuous use of the horn, with it quite understood that no one moves a hair until the last possible moment, and then only a fraction of the distance I would move. We saw several accidents, but clipped only one chicken ourselves.

We arrived in Wuhu after five, but luckily a Chinese friend who spoke English had returned after-hours to the Hong Kong travel office I called. He instantly agreed to make all the rearrangements I requested.

Next morning party leaders, the young people and surgeons who had made our visit memorable and my own group were all gathered in the hall outside my room as I emerged to a moving farewell. The hospital sent Margaret and me in the hospital car the three-hour drive to Hefei with the hope we could catch the once-a-week plane to Hong Kong. First we had to cross the Yangtze. From the ferry below Ichishan we waved a last farewell.

My desk today is littered with letters from friends in China. But I know, finally, after a lifetime of feeling split and homeless, that I belong in this small town of Conway in Massachusetts, a realization that flooded over me during a celebration to honor a beloved citizen. As we sat in the community church basement filled with friends who paid tribute to her special contributions to the town throughout her long life, I realized I was one of the few outsiders present. As I thought about the one friend I found alive in my home town, I knew there was no place on earth where I can experience the depth and range of shared memories evident that night. I also felt a special contentment.

China today is not my world. I long for the raunchy, earthy, cheerful and tragic world of my childhood, but if it still existed I would be a misfit in either its Chinese or its mission communities; nor would I wish my Chinese friends the return of a world they rejected. As it was sixty and more years ago, China is still a land in which one's peers can make the difference between sufficiency and ruin, life or death, a propensity that has hardened into a system with which I would not want to live. However flawed its own ship of state, the United States is where I belong.

But neither do I feel torn by choice. My heart is here; my heart remains in China. This came clear one day when I idly picked up the police permit I had been granted to visit Wuhu in 1980 and for the first time turned it over to the back page where I discovered "Points for Attention"

I hadn't noticed before. The last read: "Having served its purpose, this Travel Permit should be submitted to local public security agents."

How delightful. Through my negligence I am, officially, still in Wuhu.

Elsie H. Landstrom

Enroute to Huang shan in 1989 we traveled by bus through southern Anhwei where my father walked the narrow dykes and somewhat larger paths. This is the countryside he knew well.

Farewell to Ichishan from ferry crossing the Yangtze in October 1989.

Epilogue

I AM SO GLAD TO SEE YOU!

— PAUL G. HAYES

We were a sorry bunch that steamed into New York harbor on the great ocean liner SS *Europa* in August 1935. Paul Libby, one of three friends who traveled with my family, was barely out of an Athens hospital following emergency surgery for a ruptured appendix that had formed an abscess on a kidney. My sister and I had picked up whooping cough in Shanghai and whooped our way through the three-month trip to New York. My mother was fighting sties in both eyes. My father was recovering from dysentery picked up in the Middle East and was on crutches with a broken ankle. He was in debt and unemployed.

Following the tedious disembarking we went our separate ways, my father hobbling to the Board of Foreign Missions in New York City to try to get a line on a job while the rest of us were scooped up by various relatives. At the Board offices the pastor of a large church in Minneapolis who had heard his story invited him to be an associate for a year, with that church sponsoring his return to China.

The Depression in the West and the unrest in China being what they were, the return never materialized, and my father joined the Minnesota Methodist Conference. His first appointment was to a charge in North Minneapolis. Its congregation was dwindling as the surrounding Jewish and Black communities grew; both district superintendent and bishop proposed to close it the following year. My father preached one sermon titled, "Our Strenuous Gospel." "Too strenuous?" he quipped, when the

188

church promptly burned down. It was a conflagration, however, that re-kindled the spirit of its congregation, and it fell to my father to recognize what had happened, to convince the powers-that-be that a viable church body existed and to lead the way to rebuild its charred edifice. The three nearby Jewish temples proved to be good neighbors throughout the eighteen months it took to rebuild. They were welcomed in return by the church on special occasions when all worshipped together. The bonds of friendship forged in that community over the next six years were strong and sustaining, many of them intact through the years and several pastorates that followed.

Starting at the bottom with this burned-out church, my father was quickly recognized for his organizing and leadership abilities. He was soon in the forefront of Twin City efforts to bring together Protestants, Catholics and Jews, quickly involved with the local and national social and political issues. Within the life of his church he became Conference Missionary Secretary for the Northern Minnesota Conference. In the Minnesota Annual Conference he served as a member of its Board of Missions and as Chairman of its interboard Commission on Social Relations. For six years he was district superintendent in its Southwest District.

In an eight-year pastoral interlude in Bismarck, North Dakota, he was also a member of the World Service and Finance Commissions of the Conference and dean of the Methodist Pastors School of the Dakotas. This last was of special interest as he always found working with younger people a delight. In later years we were never surprised when pastors dropped by to acknowledge him to have been their inspiration to the ministry.

At his memorial service a pastor who had been in Minnesota for thirty-four years told about his experience as a student pastor while at Drew. When district superintendents from across the country were making their annual recruitment visits, he had already had several interviews before he came to a small room, and "there was Dr. Hayes, a small, precise, energetic, passionate man," who said, "Charles, this conversation is not just between you and me. It is between God, you and me. It is about your call to the ministry. We need to pray together." Charles went on to address the rows of other pastors at the memorial service, telling them how he had gone to find his wife to tell her they were going to Minnesota. "And Paul Hayes kept track of me for the past thirty-four years, just as he has kept track of each one of you."

Throughout his second term in China the resource materials my father had gathered from which to write his dissertation remained boxed. The demanding work he faced on his return to the States precluded any further attempt to tackle it. But in North Dakota he received an honorary Doctorate of Divinity from Wesley College, University of North Dakota.

Back in Minnesota he was appointed to directorates in the Rochester Methodist Hospital, the Paul Watkins Home in Winona, to Old Frontenac Point Camp in Frontenac, and to the Methodist Hospital in Minneapolis.

He had the vision to see a need and the abilities to create an organization to fill that need and to get it up and running on a sound track. These capabilities had flowered in his youth at the Water Street Mission and with the founding and first pastorate of Ross Street Church in Lancaster. In Minnesota he was instrumental in the founding of the Paul Watkins Methodist Home and the Fellowship Church in Austin.

During the years immediately preceding his retirement, which he delayed as long as church regulations permitted, we watched his face droop as he believed he would become redundant. But younger pastors recognized his skills and his energy and invited him into associate pastorates, where for the next seventeen years he continued to teach adult Bible classes and to do pastoral visiting, two aspects of the ministry he especially loved.

When he retired for the third and last time in 1978 at the age of eighty-eight, he launched into the review of his life story that I had urged. This review restored to some measure a sense of his own worth that had been damaged by his having had to turn away from China and from the seminary teaching he had so strenuously prepared for. I hoped he could die while in the midst of these reflections, but it was not to be.

He lost his hearing, then the sight in one eye followed by that of the second. As my sister and I watched our parents walk off down the hall of Walker Home in Minneapolis where they had finally, protestingly, had to move, we saw two small bent figures gallantly trying to cope with their frailties. Mother died in 1988, my father six years later. He was 103.

As I watched my parents' generation of missionaries, I came to believe that those in Africa, India and China, perhaps elsewhere as well, died or returned to their home countries very soon, or they had the resiliency to live into their nineties and beyond. The strengths of body and spirit that had served my father well in China betrayed him toward the end of his life into pain of body and a spirit aggrieved.

But he never stopped greeting everyone he met, whether friend, nurse, family member, bishop or handyman with a big smile and "I am so glad to see you!" spoken, one knew, from his heart.

At the memorial service for Paul Goodman Hayes those hymns were sung and scriptures read that he had chosen. The Twin City pastors sang in chorus a favorite hymn, and his bishop spoke of "this good man, so well named," a man of "faithfulness, grace, good sense, and courage."

From the time of its composition in the 1930s he had used the Korean Creed in preference to any other as his statement of faith, and asked that it be used at his service. In 1971, always ready to update the documents of his church, he had changed the phrase in it, "Father of all," to "Parent of all humanity," acknowledging the rightness of emerging sensibilities.

The pastor conducting his memorial service told me that he had been deluged with requests to speak for Paul Hayes. Indeed there were many fine things said and many laughs in remembrance of his foibles, at which he himself had also laughed. And someone told the story about the woman at his ninety-eighth birthday party who drew up close to him to be heard and said, "I was in your Bible class for twenty-five years." She received the smiling response, "Then you must know something!"

Among those to speak at the service was my father's lawyer. As a young man he had been inspired by my father and in those final years took on, with no recompense, the financial management of my father's affairs. He asked permission to read parts of my father's will at the service.

"Paul Hayes nearly always had the last word," he commented, to ripples of laughter, " and in this document I only assisted." He went on to remark that while some of us might find writing a will distasteful, "Paul Hayes relished it. It is a wonderful document, more a testament to his faith than a will, truly a last will and testament. I have never before drawn up such a will."

My father proclaimed at the start that his most precious possession was "my experience of salvation through God's grace as expressed through the life and teachings of Jesus Christ." He thanked the 150 volunteers from his church who had helped him in many ways. He highlighted his debt to his parents who at his baptism had dedicated him to the service of God, a dedication renewed by his mother when his father died. He expressed his gratitude to his mother for her support of his decision to become a missionary, a decision that could have caused her hardship.

When he came to his worldly possessions he asked us who were family members to realize that these gifts came from both our parents, for Mother had worked side by side with him through sixty-six years of marriage. Beyond the family he listed nine church and school groups that had helped him develop his ministry, and chose six from many organizations to which he had contributed "in my tithing ministry," and bequeathed a portion to each.

He was yet the exhorter, urging those of us who might hear his will read to pass his faith on to the next generation. And he hoped we would share his conviction in making charitable contributions that the purposes of God were "a combination of one worldwide religious fellowship based on faith, hope and love, and a secular community exhibiting goodwill, cooperation and peace."

Soon after Mother died my father became very ill and was not expected to live. When I asked that the transfusions sustaining him be stopped, according to his own wishes, his doctors agreed, and said they would keep him alive until I could reach him to say good-bye. When I arrived I was met with his smile and "I am so glad to see you!" He knew why I had come and for several hours we talked and he lapsed into dream only to wake periodically to try to struggle to his feet. He wanted to meet his Lord half way. To everyone's amazement, that remarkable strength of body and spirit rallied and carried him through another six years.

When he finally got up and made that last walk to meet his Lord, I am sure his face broke into its wide smile as he said, "I am so glad to see you!"

Bill Forbes

Elsie Hayes Landstrom, former editor on the staff of the American Friends Service Committee and MIT, and senior editor with Word Guild, is retired and living in Conway, Massachusetts. In her retirement she has edited two books about her childhood China friend, Dr. Hyla S. Watters, and has plunged into watercolor painting.

Titles Available from QED Press

Biography

Hyla Doc: Surgeon in China through War and Revolution, 1924-1949, *edited by Elsie Landstrom*

 The memoirs of a dedicated healer who served through revolution, war with Japan, and civil war.

$12.95   310 pages (paper)   6" x 9"   0-936609-19-2

Hyla Doc in Africa, 1950-1961, *edited by Elsie Landstrom*

 Hyla Doc brings her unique blend of medical skill and compassion to the bush country of Liberia.

$10.50   104 pages (paper)   6" x 9"   0-936609-32-X

Poetry

Matéria Solar / Solar Matter *by Eugénio de Andrade*
Bilingual edition. Translated by Alexis Levitin

 Stunning poems by one of Europe's most famous writers in "Alexis Levitin's sensitive and lyrical translation."

$12.95   128 pages (paper) $5^1/_2$" x 7"   0-936609-34-6

A Mendocino Portfolio *by Cynthia Frank & Hannes Krebs*
 Stark poetry and evocative black and white photography.

$17.95   88 pages (case)   10" x 8"   0-936609-12-5

Another Name for Earth / O Otro Nome da Terra (bilingual)
by Eugénio de Andrade / Translated by Alexis Levitin

 New work by the celebrated Portuguese lyrical poet.

$12.95   128 pages (paper) $5^1/_2$" x 7"   0-936609-37-0

Messages: New and Selected Poems *by Luke Breit*

 Poetry highly praised by Ernesto Cardenal and Norman Mailer.

$8.95   136 pages (paper) $5^1/_2$" x $8^1/_2$"   0-936609-17-6

Psychology/Counseling/Health

Finding the Way Home: A Compassionate Approach to Illness

by Gayle Heiss

Anyone touched by health concerns will treasure *Finding the Way Home*. The inner world of illness is portrayed with clarity and compassion. A guide to living wisely, no matter one's state of health.

$24.95   320 pages (case)   6" x 9"   0-936609-35-4

Defending Against the Enemy: Coping with Parkinson's Disease

by Eric Morgan

Scientist Eric Morgan and his wife both suffered from the "enemy," Parkinson's Disease. A journal of the years "at war" coupled with scientific research, medical experimentation and practical advice.

$12.95   128 pages (paper) $5\frac{1}{2}$" x $8\frac{1}{2}$"   0-936609-36-2

Listening with Different Ears: Counseling People Over 60

by James Warnick

A practical guide for therapists, social workers, ministers and family members who want to help seniors in emotional distress.

$19.50   224 pages (paper)   6" x 9"   0-936609-28-1
$24.95   224 pages (case)   6" x 9"   0-936609-31-1

The Collected Works of Lydia Sicher: An Adlerian Perspective

Adele K. Davidson edits this definitive work of one whose "contribution to Individual Psychology is enormous and brilliant."

— *Dr. Harold Mosak, Adler School of Professional Psychology*

$24.95   572 pages (paper)   6" x 9"   0-936609-22-2

Art

Paris Connections: African American Artists in Paris

For this book, editors Asake Bomani and Belvie Rooks won a *Before Columbus Foundation American Book Award*. Bilingual (French/English), full-color reproductions, biographies, bibliography, index.

$30.00   128 pages (paper) $8\frac{1}{2}$" x 10"   0-936609-25-7

Paris Connections: African and Caribbean Artists in Paris

Editors Asake Bomani and Belvie Rooks present another collection of bilingual (French/English) essays on African and Caribbean artists in Paris. Full-color reproductions, biographies, index.

$14.95   64 pages (paper) $8\frac{1}{2}$" x $8\frac{1}{2}$"   0-936609-26-5

Creative Nonfiction

Iron House by Jerome Washington

Winner of the 1994 *Western States Arts Federation Book Award for Creative Nonfiction,* this much-praised book about the "con artists, sex addicts, psychotics and dreamers" who inhabit our prisons is both funny and searing.

$18.95   176 pages (case)   5½" x 8½"   0-936609-33-8

Fiction

Tales From The Mountain by Miguel Torga

Ivana Carlsen translates this extraordinary collection of powerful short stories by Portugal's Nobel Prize nominee.

$12.99   160 pages (paper)   5½" x 8½"   0-936609-23-0
$21.99   160 pages (case)   5½" x 8½"   0-936609-24-9

The Long Reach by Susan Davis

A different kind of science fiction story. Star-crossed lovers search for one another on Earth and in Space from deep past to distant future.

$12.95   208 pages (paper)   5½" x 8½"   0-936609-27-3

The Man Who Owned the Hogs by Leonard Dugger

A savage, elegant, iconoclastic satire that attacks the foundations of religion while telling a gripping, ultimately tragic story.

$21.95   208 pages (case)   5½" x 8½"   1-879384-18-3

Business

Take This Job and Sell It! The Recruiter's Handbook by Richard Mackie

Richard Mackie, guru to headhunters, describes, step-by-step, how to earn $100,000 a year at home by recruiting and placing professionals at mid-sized companies.

$24.95   176 pages (paper)   8½" x 11"   0-936609-30-3

Available at your local bookstore or from
QED Press
155 Cypress Street, Fort Bragg, CA 95437
(800) 773-7782 or (707) 964-9520
Fax (707) 964-7531
e-mail: qedpress@mcn.org
website: cypresshouse.com